"Hekate"

by Krysta S. Roy

Bearing Torches

A Devotional Anthology for Hekate

Edited by Sannion and the Editorial Board
of the Bibliotheca Alexandrina

BIBLIOTHECA ALEXANDRINA

I invoke you, beloved Hekate of the Crossroads and the Three Ways
Saffron-cloaked Goddess of the Heavens, the Underworld and the Sea
Tomb-frequenter, mystery-raving with the souls of the dead
Daughter of Perses, Lover of the Wilderness who exults among
   the deer
Nightgoing One, Protectress of dogs, Unconquerable Queen
Beast-roarer, Dishevelled One of compelling countenance
Tauropolos, Keyholding Mistress of the whole world
Ruler, Nymph, Mountain-wandering Nurturer of youth.
Maiden, I beg you to be present at these sacred rites
Ever with a gladsome heart and ever gracious to the Oxherd.

- *Orphic Hymn to Hekate*

Now it is the time of night
That the graves all gaping wide,
Every one lets forth his sprite,
In the church-way paths to glide:
And we fairies, that do run
By the triple Hecate's team,
From the presence of the sun,
Following darkness like a dream,
Now are frolic: not a mouse
Shall disturb this hallow'd house:
I am sent with broom before,
To sweep the dust behind the door.

- William Shakespeare, *A Midsummer Night's Dream*, 5.1

Gone are the leaves on the Hecate trees
Shed to the wind till her skeleton claws the sky
I am alone in a forest of memory
Dragging behind me the howl of the winter

Hecate,
Hecate,
Hecate.

- Wendy Rule, *"Hecate"*

To you, Hekate, the community gives this book full of love and beauty.
May it be pleasing to your heart!

Acknowledgements

Many thanks to:

Diotima, for all her help in the initial stages.

Kate Winter, for making this book as organized and lovely as it is.

The good folks at Neos Alexandria, without whose talent and dedication this book would never have come to be. I'll miss working with you guys!

Table of Contents

Introduction

It's a chill November evening as I write these words. Dead leaves litter the streets, the smell of their decay perfuming the air. There's something else in the air as well, a crispness, a tenseness as the world prepares for the long, dead winter months that are about to descend upon us.

This time of year has always felt pregnant with the spirit of Hekate for me. Her torches are reflected in the brilliant reds and oranges of the leaves as they fall – one last brilliant display of color before they are transformed into the mulch that feeds the earth and the tree that shall be reborn with vibrant greens come spring. Her kiss is the icy breeze that whips our face, forcing us to bury our hands in coat pockets as we walk a little faster, eager for the warmth of our homes. Her voice is the growl of a hungry dog digging in the trash for a desperate last meal. If it fails to find it, the next morning will discover its fragile, forgotten corpse on the side of the road, food for some other creature.

Hekate is a strange and powerful goddess, a force of primal transformation. She is hunger and longing and dark mystery. She is also beautiful if you have an eye to see it, and kind in her way – though there is no sentimentality to her kindness. She is willing to help, but only if you're willing to do your part as well. She won't coddle, and she cuts through all of our excuses with a severity that sometimes seems cruel. In truth, that's usually just the thing we need to jar us out of our comfortable complacency.

The ancient Greeks recognized this about her. She was never one of the familiar Olympian deities, but they gave her an honored place nonetheless, for the world isn't always a safe, sunlit place. There are shadows and dangers and things that fit outside of our expectations. And this is where Hekate can be found – on the outside: in the yard, protecting the home, at the crossroads with the vagrants, dogs, and ghosts, in the semi-barbaric lands to the north of Greece where men are wild and women are witches.

Hekate haunts our dreams and the fertile places of imagination. She alone of all the gods could travel easily between the worlds of the dead, the living, and the divine. And she has come through the centuries to be with us today. Though a marginal goddess at best in antiquity, Hekate is one of the most popular goddesses in the pagan revival going on today. You will find both Hellenic Recons and Wiccans praying to her. Thanks to Shakespeare, even people who have never poured out a libation know her name.

The wide appeal of the goddess is borne out in the following essays, poems, short stories, and accounts of personal experiences which fill the pages of this book. Each of them has a fascinating story to tell and a personal vision of Hekate which may differ from person to person. We have allowed each of our contributors to speak in their own words and describe the Hekate that they know. Therefore you will find Hekate as the dark crone and the lovely maiden, as the guide of souls and protector of the home, as the mistress of magic and a promoter of fertility in fields and flocks. All of these are authentic visions of Hekate, for she is an immense goddess and complex as they come. Whether or not you see the Hekate you know reflected in these accounts, one thing that will hopefully be clear is the great respect and love that we all have for this goddess. A book like this could not be produced without that kind of devotion, and thus I am proud to offer to the venerable goddess the accumulated offerings of her community. Ie Hekate!

Sannion aka H. Jeremiah Lewis
Eugene, Oregon
3 November, 2009

Editorial Note

Throughout this book you will find the name of the goddess alternately written as Hekate and Hecate. Both are acceptable and popular forms. The first is an attempt to render an accurate transliteration of the Greek Ἑκάτη into English, while the second adopts the Latinized version which was used throughout the Roman Empire and in Classical circles until fairly recently. Different authors have different associations with these spellings, and therefore we have kept them as originally written in the individual pieces. Likewise, there are a number of unusual epithets associated with the goddess. These are explained at the end of the book.

The Key Bearer

by Michael Routery

I see you on the stairway with a flashlight
Dangling a huge ring of keys, formidable and ancient,
Going down to your locked basement packed with secrets.
They say your mien was once much more pleasant
(but isn't that true of all?).
Out of peripheral vision
You seem dog-like,
Your head elongating and tripling.
I inhale sharply, enshadowed;
I know to be careful around here:
This building conceals an underworld gate.
So I construct a *hekataion* on the front steps
And sweep out shed cat-hair,
Dust and pollen early in the mornings.
One day I find a gift of sparkling glass,
Shards artificed into a delicate bracelet
And in the center a heart of green glass glimmers,
A light for my lantern when I descend the staircase
To where the beast growls behind the bars.

Finding My Way to Hekate

by John Drury

May the Goddess be pleased with this story.

My journey to Hekate has not been a simple one, and the telling of it requires the telling of my own story first. Readers, I hope, will grant their patience in this telling.

Years ago, in sixth grade and in a small elementary school south of the Mason-Dixon line, a kindly and elderly librarian taught all of the students in that grade about Greek mythology. I of course took the class as well, and arrived at the awards ceremony at the end of the school year eager to see how I'd done in the class. Parents were invited, and my mother attended. As awards were handed out to the best students, I received my grade: an F. I came in last in the class. When I inquired to the librarian, her response was that I hadn't turned in much work and that "some things are just not meant for certain people." She meant, of course, that I was obviously not suited to studying Greek myth.

She was wrong.

In college, I received a Bachelor of Arts with a double major in History in Political Science, and a minor in Classical Studies. The history field of study was the Greeks, from the time of the Minoans through the Ottoman Empire. Thus, not only was I exposed to history, but also to the art, mythology, and language of ancient Greece. Though I had to obtain the last Greek class after graduation, I did obtain my minor and am proud of the work that I've done. I went on to get an international MBA, and did extensive studies on my own on Indo-European grammar and comparative mythology.

Yet, throughout this time, Hekate never appeared to me or held my interest. In truth, while I could name a number of gods and goddesses in both the Greek and Roman pantheon, Hekate was not one of them.

As the years passed I found myself learning of paganism and, after some years on a pagan forum, decided to begin studies in witchcraft and general neo-pagan thought and practice. I found a teacher and group with a structured study and began attending. It was then that Hekate first came to my attention. As a goddess of witches, especially in modern neo-pagan thought, Hekate's importance is quite strong for many neo-pagan groups and practices. I received general instruction on how many neo-pagans invoked, or worked with, Hekate. Still, in our group, we had a generic 'god and goddess' and did not emphasize individual deities. Additionally, most of the work we did was 'low magick' and not usually associated with deities. It was good material, taught well, but it provided only a foundation for craft practices. The next step, the work with and worship of deity, was left to the individual students to pursue on their own.

It was at this point that the Greek gods began to assert themselves in my life. It should come as no surprise that the Greek gods were the first to make their presence known. Looking back on it, They were always there, simply waiting for me to become aware of Them. Dionysos was the first, He who often is a gateway deity. The Dioskouroi, for reasons I've never really understood, are strong in my personal pantheon. But it was not until Persephone crept into my conscious understanding that Hekate appeared. It was then that I re-read the old myths concerning Demeter and Persephone, and saw Hekate's role in them. Though she had not called to me directly, I knew that it was time to begin the process of knowing the goddess and giving Her the due She deserves.

Many modern neo-pagans begin their studies by learning of the sabbats and esbats. The first, involving the eight 'High Holidays' are based on solar events such as the equinoxes. The esbats, on the other hand, are times of magick, as they correspond to the full and dark moons. Hekate, I knew from class, was often associated with the dark moon and with the mysteries of magickal practices. Imagine my surprise when I, again, learnt of her more complex nature. A goddess of witchcraft emerged as a goddess associated with childbirth, the dead, crossroads, and a strong companion of Persephone and Demeter. As with Nemesis and Tyche, she can bestow fortune (good or ill) upon humans. In short, her complex nature and strong chthonic powers came to the fore, and I found myself hoping to establish some relationship and cultus with this goddess.

Fortunately, both ancient and modern neo-pagan practices merge here. For it is the end of the lunar month, on the dark moon, that Hekate's deipnon is celebrated. It is a time to make offerings, to clean the house and self of things to be discarded, and give them to Hekate instead. For some time I had wondered what to do to celebrate some of the esbats. The deipnon gives a clear purpose, and a ready-made avenue to work with Hekate regardless of the path you're on or where you started. It was thus that I celebrated my first deipnon in the early Summer of 2009. I prepared a meal of discarded food, and after creating ritual space I introduced myself to the goddess and asked for her cleansing powers in the home in return for the food offerings. It was a powerful experience, done at night, and walking to the crossroads with the offering and leaving it there in silence left a lasting impression.

In my own unverified personal gnosis, I believe that Persephone leaves the world at Mabon (or the Autumnal Equinox) and returns at Ostara (the Spring Equinox). It was thus gratifying in 2009 to see the dark moon fall within a couple of days of the Autumnal equinox. Not only did I prepare a small but full meal for Hekate, I made specific prayers for her to accompany Persephone on her journey, and to provide counsel during this time. I also asked that we humans not be forgotten in these dark times, and that her two torches lead us when we need them. It was by torchlight, soon after, that I conducted a ritual farewell for Persephone and a recitation for the dead. I asked Hekate to assist, as her purview of the dead overlaps that of Hermes, Nemesis, and Persephone. I believe that the deipnons during the Winter months will be the more powerful ones, and I look forward to them with enthusiasm.

Hail bright-coiffed Hekate, goddess of magic, of the dead, of the crossroads. May your torches shine like beacons, and light the way for those mortals who seek your counsel and assistance.

Hecate in My Life

by Allyson Szabo

When I was 19, I was living in Vancouver, BC (Canada) with my Wiccan priest, Davydd, happily learning how to be a good Wiccan. I enjoyed what I was learning, and at the time, I think it was the best thing I could have done. I learned a lot through Davydd's lessons, about myself and about the world around me. When the time approached for my First Degree, Davydd suggested a series of meditations designed to allow me to connect with a "matron goddess," if I had one. While Wicca has its own deities, it does not deny the existence of others, and Davydd felt it was important to give me an opportunity to find out where my allegiances lay. Of course, I complied.

During my meditations, I kept running into a spiritual brick wall. I would consistently be taken back to a single face, a single goddess. I saw her as being somewhat ageless, not really being "maid, mother, or crone" as one would expect in the Wiccan paradigm. I did not know at first who she was; I knew only that she scared the bejeezus out of me and I wanted nothing to do with her. Davydd suggested that I explore what she had to offer, but I refused outright.

After some time, I learned that it was Hecate who was appearing to me. This confused me further because I had always heard Hecate was old, the "crone aspect," and yet this woman was not old in the least. I knew she was the "goddess of witches" and that she was a "dark goddess." Because I was neglecting my homework and ignoring her advances, I really didn't know much else about her. She was persistent, though, and would not take no for an answer.

Some days after my First Degree ritual was over, I was engaging in a series of repetitive meditations that I practice. I visualized myself as an owl, and I soared through the night sky, skimming over trees and through a forest, hunting and searching. Normally, this meditation was very calming, and ended with the capture of a fat mouse or vole, and I would end the meditation before the "feast" began. Not that day, though!

The visualization started out as usual. It was a waning moon, and the sky was quite dim, with only a scattering of far-off stars and a mere sliver of moon casting a bit of light. From an owl's perspective, though, it was as bright as day. I had just spied something moving below me, and focused on it, when my world was turned upside down.

Suddenly, it was no longer night, and cool, and relaxing. It was the middle of the day, with a burning sun beating on my feathers. The wind was all different, being dry and hot instead of moist and cool. I started to panic as I realized that the feathers were not *my* feathers, and I had no idea how to steer this particular body!

I felt myself plummeting, a sensation that has always bothered me since my early childhood. I couldn't breathe, and I was flapping for all I was worth. Then the body reflexes took over, and I was no longer flapping and diving. I was soaring, and the whole world spread out below me. A large canyon was what I was flying over, but I could see for miles, the red, dry earth stretching away into the curve of the planet itself. That's when I heard the whistle, and instinct took over. I folded those lovely, strong wings, so different from the owl's soft wings, and I dived, down down down, toward a single point where the sound had come from. With barely a ruffle of those stiff, brownish red feathers, I settled onto the arm of the woman I had so fervently been trying to avoid.

To my extreme embarrassment, she hooded me, blinded me with a leather cap, and then fed me. She made the soothing sounds that one makes to a strong and well behaved pet. I found myself preening, leaning into her finger strokes, happy to be where I was. It was then that I realized I would never be free of this very strong goddess, and that I would always be her creature. That was in 1991, I believe, and I've been her creature ever since.

Over the years, I have learned a lot more about the goddess who has taken me as her servant. While she does have her scary moments, and at rare moments has appeared to me in an older guise, she is usually very timeless in her appearance. For me, she often arrives in robes that are dark yellow or red in color, which I later learned were her usual colors. She is sometimes called "the saffron-robed goddess" in the traditional poems. She has her connections with magic and witches, both ancient and modern. Her worship was often performed at a crossroads, where three roads came together. She has much to do with death and pain, and other things that the Olympic gods have no interest in.

Hecate is originally a Thracian goddess, not a Greek one. There is quite a bit of evidence to support the idea that she was worshipped in a similar way to Hestia, being a goddess of hearth and home. When she joined the Olympic gods, she lost much of her home connections. However, many homes still had small altars or shrines to her at their front door, and offerings were left to her there every month at the new moon. New moon offerings of food were also left at crossroads, well into the modern historical era. She is often depicted with hunting hounds, and with hawks and owls. There are mythological connections between Hecate and Artemis, strangely enough. And Hecate maintains her position as protector of the pregnant woman, and of newborn children. Even Zeus himself was said to have gone to her for advice.

My own experiences with Hecate have been wide and varied. I have memories of being quite young, around 7 or 8 years old, and being embraced by a female deity who I simply thought of as "god" at the time, but who I now believe was Hecate. She has been a constant in my life, always with me through the various changes and moves that I have made. Through her graces, I have been present at two deaths, where I gently directed the souls of the departed onward, and it is something that I consider very important. I seem often to have tasks to do that deal with death and grief, and it doesn't seem to bother me as much as it does others.

I am pleased to be a priestess of Hecate. I have always felt very close to her, and she has been a vital part of my life. It was her involvement in my life that I believe short circuited my "fluffy" phase, something that happens to a lot of Wiccans early on. I never held the belief that everything was light and wonderful, and I have always embraced the dark that comes along with and enhances the light.

She Meets Me at the Crossroads and Shows Me the Way

by Krysta S. Roy

In dewy mists of darkest night
On the plain of dreams I roam
Answering the call of victorious Sleep
Who fought my insomnia and won.
Tears streaming down my cheeks
I come to a tree with twisted limbs
Where a spider spins her silken web
Shimmering in the dim star light.
Incomplete, unfinished, not yet set in place
Much like my own destiny.
The story is not finished, not over
There is still more to be done.
But I do not see it, do not realize
And so I pass it by.

I come to a hill on which a black dog sits
Howling at a pale crescent Moon
The wailing echoing my broken heart
Mourning and tortured, shattered
Screaming to the heavens
I cannot take much more.
In the distance the dog hears an answering song
Another voice reaching out into the night.
Comforted that he is not alone
He moves towards its source.
But I do not see it, do not realize
And again I pass it by.

I come to a bed set upon the clouds
A full Moon shining high above.
I fall upon it weeping
And curl myself in a ball.
A snake twists itself at the edge of the mattress
Into the shape of infinity.
This pain is not all there is
There can still be so much more.
But I do not see it, do not realize
I turn my head, avert my eyes
Surrendering to my pain
Gathering the broken shards of my soul around me.

And then the snake coils, its patience spent
And strikes, biting into my flesh.
The venom flows like fire through my veins...
And then I finally see
Then I finally realize.
She stands before me in indigo robes
The stars themselves adorn her
And with her torches held high
She illuminates the darkness.
My bed sits in the center of the crossroads
I turn and see the road I've walked behind.
She stretches her arms open wide
And nods her head towards each fiery torch.

Then I see in the blazing fire light
Two roads ahead I had not seen before.
"You were meant to do more than this," she says
Her gaze now meeting mine
"Will you let this beat you and keep you down?
Or will you trust in me and rise?"
She places her torches in the bedposts
And reaches her hands out to me
In a silent challenge I cannot refuse.
I put my hands in hers
Trembling, shaking, terrified
As she pulls me to my feet.

"Fear is not a weakness," she says
"But courage is moving forward through it
Moving forward despite it.
If you will walk, I will be beside you."
I take the first stumbling step forward
And choose a new path to walk
The edge of the road glimmering
Like stardust in her torchlight.
My heart pounds like a frantic drum
As I step into the mists
Her hand still holding mine
And when I wake, the tears have dried.

A Triad for Hekate

by Rebecca Buchanan

I. *Thrice-Beautiful*

Deep is my delight
Great is my dread
For I have seen Your face
Thrice-Beautiful Hekate

II. *Terrible Hekate*

I am Terrible Hekate
I walk dark moon nights
I speak for the dead
       Hear their voices.

III. *Thracian*

Thrice-Great Goddess
Graced with the head of
       dog
       and horse
       and triple-tongued serpent
Who travels with the moon tides
Collecting offerings at the crossroads
       sweet honey
       and black lambs
       and newborn puppies
Who grants or withholds at your whim
       the blessings of sea
       and sky
       and earth
Thracian
Thrice-Great Goddess
Grant me a boon!

Who is Hekate?

by Amanda Sioux Blake

If one were to ask who the most popular Goddess in the broad spectrum of modern Paganism was, Hekate would certainly be a prominent contender, if not the ultimate winner. Yet there are as many different conceptions of this Goddess as there are worshipers. Wiccans may tell you that She is a Crone Goddess, part of the Grecian Triple Goddess, with Artemis as Maiden/waxing moon, Selene as Mother/full moon, and Hekate as Crone/waning and dark moon.

Yet this image varies greatly from that of ancient Greece. Although Hekate is often pictured in triplicate form, She is not a Triple Goddess. She was not seen as a Crone, either, but as a comely young woman who presided over the crossroads, particularly wherever three roads meet. Some even maintained that Hekate was a virgin Goddess,[1] although others believed that She was the mother of the sea-monster Skylla,[2] and others the mother of the famous witches Medea and Kirke.[3] Hekate is a Goddess of magic, wisdom, the night, ghosts and the Underworld – all things Wiccans associate with the Crone aspect of their Goddess, so the confusion is understandable. Similarly Selene is not a Mother Goddess. She is a Goddess who happens to be a mother, but She is not a Mother. That is, She does not fulfill the role of Mother Goddess to humanity. This does not mean that either of these Goddesses do not currently manifest as such to their Wiccan followers, merely these concepts where not held in ancient Greece, where these deities were first worshiped.

Hekate is a diverse Goddess, with many functions. She is usually the child of the Titans Perses and Asteria,[4] or Perses and Persaios.[5] However, another text mentions Hekate as being a daughter of Nyx,[6] the ancient Goddess of Night whom even Zeus stood in awe of. Nyx being Hekate's mother would most certainly explain Her power.

But whatever Her parentage, Hekate was one of the most powerful, respected and sometimes feared Goddesses of Greece. She alone has a power shared with Zeus – that of granting or withholding from humanity anything She wishes. While She never joined the Olympian company, Zeus honored Her above all other deities (except Nyx) by giving Her a special place and granting Her dominion over heaven, earth, and the underworld. According to Hesiod She became a bestower of wealth and all blessings of everyday life, and in the human sphere She rules over the great mysteries of birth, life, and death. A cursory reading of the *Theogony* will make it clear that Hesiod was

21

especially devoted to Hekate. In the middle of his genealogy of the Gods, he goes on quite a long tangent discussing the many qualities and blessings of Hekate, taking on an almost televangelist-like tone.

She is associated with childbirth and prophetic visions as well. She is a guide of souls into the Underworld, a complement to the male psychopomp, Hermes. Like Hermes, She is a boundary Goddess. Many Hellenes had an image of Her next to the front door of their home,[7] so She would protect the home and stop any evil influences from entering. She is the Goddess of the crossroads, where ancient magic typically took place under cover of night. When in three forms looking in three directions, She can see the past, presence and the future. Her sacred animals are the weasel or polecat[8] and dogs,[9] especially hunting dogs. In fact She is often called Lady of Hounds and Nurse of Puppies, and Nonnus in his *Dionysiaca* referred to Hekate as "the divine friend of dogs."[10] One of Her greatest symbols are torches, two of which She is often pictured holding. Hekate carried torches while She assisted Demeter with the search for Her kidnapped daughter Persephone, and earned Herself a place in the Eleusinian Mysteries as the guide of initiates.

Later traditions make Hekate the daughter of Zeus and Asteria[11] and reduce Her power to only that of the Underworld, childbirth and the waning to dark moon. By Roman times She became chiefly understood as the Goddess of the dark moon, crossroads, witchcraft and ghosts.

Because Her nature was originally that of a mysterious and somewhat unknowable deity, more prominence was given in classical times to Her gloomy or appalling aspects. The classical Greeks emphasized Hekate's destructive powers at the expense of Her creative one, until at last She was invoked only as Goddess of the netherworld and secret rites of black magic and necromancy, especially in places where three roads met in the darkness of night.

The Greeks' image of Hekate may have been influenced by the Egyptian Goddess Heqit or Heket. Heqit is pictured as a frog-headed woman, and was believed to be the midwife who assisted with the daily birth of the Sun. She is a Goddess of creation and germination of seeds into plants. In Her connection to childbirth we see where Her sphere and that of Hekate intersects. Frogs are sometimes considered a symbol of Hekate as well. Another intriguing connection to Egypt is the Egyptian concept of Heka, roughly translated as magic.

Although many deities of both Greek and Egyptian origin were invoked in ancient spells and curses, the two Gods most often associated with magic in the Greek mind were Hermes and Hekate.[12] Hekate is a very complex Goddess, much more than just a Goddess of magic, but by Roman times Her magical aspects had swallowed up the other sides to Her, and She became the witches' Goddess that we know today. Hermes Trismegestos, the "Thrice-Greatest," evolved to become a God of alchemy during the Renaissance.

It is appropriate that Hermes and Hekate have a close relationship. It's said that an Underworld Goddess by the name of Brimo gave Her virginity to Hermes, sleeping with Him on the banks of the Lake Boibeis in Thessaly,[13] an area known in classical times for its high concentration of witches and magic. Brimo, meaning "Angry" or "Terrifying," was an epithet of Hekate. It was also a title of both Demeter and Persephone. In this case Demeter is an unlikely interpretation. Persephone would perhaps have been justifiable, if the text in question had not said that this Brimo had been a virgin when She lay with Hermes. So these two Deities most often associated with magic come to have an intimate relationship.

In Greece, Hekate was a pre-Olympic Goddess, possibly a native of Thrake, in the northeast part of the country. Unlike many other primordial deities, Hekate was absorbed into the classical Greek pantheon. And when the Romans absorbed Hekate into their pantheon along with the other Greek Gods, they did not even change Her name, merely Latinizing the spelling to Hecate.

Hekate is one of those deities who greatly intrigued me from a young age, but with whom I have had little contact. When I first began worshiping Pagan Gods, Artemis, Athena and Hekate were the deities who drew me the most. I appealed to Hekate mostly as Goddess of magic and divination. While I no longer practice magic, I still appeal to the Gods on occasion for divination – through Tarot, astrology, and a few private forms I created myself. I am not a devotee of Hekate, and I have not had a major experience of Her quite some time. Still, I look on my memories of Her with fondness.

She is a fierce and independent Goddess. Although not a virgin like Artemis, with whom She is often associated, Hekate is wild and free. At a time in my life when I was overly worried about the opinions of my peers, Hekate forced me to work on myself. She didn't care what others thought of me, and was very insistent that I should not either. Hekate can be very harsh at times, but She is never harsh without reason. She teaches us some hard but necessary lessons. Everything that is broken, lost or discarded belongs to Her. She takes the broken soul to Her, and forges it into something stronger, something better. She demands strength, She demands sacrifice. And the rewards, if you live up to Her expectations, are beyond imagining. After being tested by this Goddess, you will emerge stronger, more confidant, trusting in your own strengths and intuition. You will have a new steel in your soul, and Hekate will sit back and nod approvingly while you take on the world, completely on your own.

1. Apollonius Rhodius 3.840, Lycophron 1174
2. Apollonius Rhodius 4.827
3. Diodorus Siculus 4.45.1
4. Hesiod. *Theogony* 404 , Apollodorus 1.8
5. Homeric Hymn 2 to Demeter. 24, Apollonius Rhodius. 3.1036, Diodorus Siculus. 4.45.1, Ovid. *Metamorphoses* 7.74, Seneca. *Medea* 812
6. Greek Lyric IV Bacchylides, Frag 1B, Scholiast on Apollonius Rhodius. 3.467
7. Aristophanes. *Wasps* 804 ff, Euripides. *Medea* 396 ff, Aeschylus, Fragment 216 (from Scholiast on Theocritus, Idyll 2. 36)
8. Antoninus Liberalis. *Metamorphoses* 29, Aelian. *On Animals* 15.11
9. Apollonius Rhodius. *Argonautica* 3.1194, Lycophron. *Alexandra* 1174 , Ovid. *Metamorphoses* 10.403 , Virgil. *Aeneid* 6.257, Nonnus. *Dionysiaca* 44.198, Valerius Flaccus. *Argonautica* 6.110
10. Nonnus. *Dionysiaca* 3.61
11. Scholiast on Apollonius Rhodius 3.467 ap Musaeus
12. Diodorus Siculus. *Library of History* 4.45.1, Ovid. *Metamorphoses* 6.139, Seneca. *Medea* 570
13. Propertius. *Elegies* 2.29C

Shaking the Bones

by Melitta Benu

You shake my bones.

Your names drip from my tongue like honey:

Prytania, Invincible Queen.
Khthonia, dark like the deep earth.
Brimo, your wrath like the rolling thunder.

In the silence of my secret self,
I reach for you –
Womb of the World
Who cycles our souls,
Resurrected,
Renewed.

Theurgist, Witch Queen, Night Walker –
You dance among the dead
Like a yew wet with falling rain,
Like a charmed serpent,
Like a festival fire brand
Cutting a path through the dark.

You shake my bones.

Your names drip from my tongue like blood:

Antania, our enemy,
Soteira, our savior,
Aidonaia, secret bride of Hades.

In the mania of my darkest self,

I reach for you–
Luminary of katabasis:
Mad Alchemist, Arcane Priestess –
The only one who knows the way
Home.

You are the poison which cures,
The pain which purifies,
The light that wanes and returns:

25

Anassa eneroi, a mystery concealed

And revealed in your own time.

You shake my bones.

Your names drip from my tongue like honey:

Megiste, Majestic and Mighty,
Atalos with a tender heart,
Beloved. Beloved. Beloved.

To Hekate

by Corbin

She stands at the crossroads under the cowl
Of the sky with goblets in all her claws.
Wind flutters her cloak, obscuring the moon,
Revealing the Book of the Laws.

Ruby wine beckons but I dare not drink
In the night with her eyes like coins of gold
Watching and her silence as ominous
And deep as the sea is old.

O seedless vision, Daughter of the Gates
Of Time, is your offer enlightenment,
Your gift illumination or demise?
Which brings the best contentment?

Kind Dark Mother, I will decline all cups,
Slip away, head bowed as in reflection.
Let me walk a bit longer in the air,
Goddess, but which direction?

Devotional Prayer to Hekate

by Antonella Vigliarolo

Dark Queen who walks among graves,
Saffron-clad, flanked by hounds and revered by ghosts,
Virginal siren who dances in between thunder and lighting, mantled
    by rain,
Coal-eyed Mistress of All Mysteries,
Wild and kind,
Fierce and wise,
Yours is the hand that severs the chord in our last hour
And ties the knot once more when we are reborn.
Yours is the torch revealing our minds' demons,
Cracking our masks beyond repair.
You are the ageless chant of mystical ecstasy,
The light and that same light's shadow.
You are the ardent gaze that delves into those subtle distances of other
    times, other places, other selves.
Most ancient maiden who mirrors in the Crone,
Darkest face of the Muse,
Midwife Divine,
Hekate Trivia,
Hekate Enodia,
Hekate Soteira,
Hekate Prytania,
Hekate Phosphoros,
Hekate Kleidophorous,
I honor You.

Hekate, the Dark Goddess

by Diotima

"Hekate, Cerridwyn, dark mother take us in, Hekate, Cerridwyn, let us be reborn" - *Hekate, Cerridwyn,* Inkubus Sukkubus

So begins the simple chant on the "Wild" album: first with a single voice, then with others added in obvious but still pleasing harmonies. The song is evocative, in most senses of the word. But, listening to it, I was moved to muse – is it accurate, at least in terms of what we know of what the Greeks thought about the goddess of the crossroads? The follow on question, of course, is whether or not such accuracy matters?

Hekate is one of those goddesses who has been adopted by many in the Neo-Pagan movement; generally as a "dark goddess," redolent of death, evil, and the underworld. How accurate is this, for one described as "bright coiffed"? As she is described as "maiden," can she really be a (or our) mother, of whatever hue? And, perhaps more importantly, does it matter if it's accurate to what the ancient Greeks thought, if it's what is thought by people now?[1]

The first question might seem straightforward: how did the Greeks view Hekate? We know she was "highly honoured" by Zeus, but what else can we say with any certainty at all? Unfortunately, as anyone who has ever really delved into the fascinating and frustrating study that is Greek mythology will know, things are rarely straightforward.

Hekate is no exception to this lack of clarity. By this I do not mean that the Greeks were unclear about her, but rather, that we are unclear about what they, themselves believed, where, and when. Partially, this is a function of not being a "people of the book" – having one, central tome – but rather being a people of many books (and poems and hymns and tablets and plays and stories and....). But mainly, it's a function of the fact that the Greeks didn't feel any *need* to come to a straightforward conclusion about who and what Hekate was, as they didn't see the point in trying to pin down even something as obvious as a human person, much less something as ephemeral as an old, old god.[2]

And Hekate is old – in the sense that she clearly predates the Olympians. She is a Titan, daughter of Titans. She is given her portion of the earth, sea and sky by the leader of the Olympians, Zeus – or to be more exact about it, she is allowed to keep what is already hers – which points again to her antiquity as a god.

In the chant mentioned above, Hekate is reckoned to be a "dark mother." And indeed, at times she is recorded as being a mother (if not dark), as being the parent of the sea monster Skylla, who so frightened the Argonauts, or even of Kirke[3] (Circe) and Medea (which, considering the fairly constant relation given between Hekate and witchcraft or magic, makes a good deal of sense). Certainly Medea counts herself as one of Hekate's priestesses, and sees Hekate as her goddess.

Unfortunately, even one of the same authors seems to fluctuate on this point, calling her "maiden" in another passage; and she is also called maiden in another source. The simple explanation, of course, is that these references are made to her before her marriage, (which may have been to Hermes or to Aeetes).

To confuse matters even more for modern readers, Hekate is sometimes associated with other deities, such as Artemis (who is at times called Hekate or Diana or Athena). At least these associations lend weight to the idea that she may have been a virgin goddess, as do the representations in which she wears the maiden's short chiton rather than a matron's longer gown. So she is seen as both maiden and mother. Any suggestion of the threefold maiden, mother, crone triplet, however, should be negated at this point: while there are numerous triple gods or gods with three (or more – often many, many more) versions or types in Greek mythology, Hekate certainly does not present anywhere as the tripartite maiden-mother-crone.

But what of the "dark goddess" image?

And does it matter?

Certainly Hekate is associated with darkness and the night, and the dead...eventually. It is possible that these associations only grew with time, as Marquardt suggests; the early mentions of her have no chthonic overtones, while by the end of the fifth century BC, in Euripides, they are certainly there .

Chthonic deities – from the Greek word meaning "earth" – were those associated with the earth, with the dark, with the underworld. For some deities, the chthonic "version" of themselves is obvious and well known: Hades, for instance, the ruler of the underworld; Kore (Persephone), who spends half of the year underground is another example. However, a "dark" side could be found to most of the well known gods – Hermes is the select messenger to Hades, designated as such by his own father, Zeus, and often functions as a psychopomp (guide of the dead) while Hermes' father Zeus also received chthonic sacrifices. Dionysus, best known today for his love of wine and revelry, has a chthonic side, as being associated with that-which-comes-from-the-ground in spring. The connection between these gods is not involvement in "dark" workings, such as curses or blood work, but rather their association with the agricultural cycle. They are "dark" because the earth – and what lies under it – are dark. "Chthonic" and "dark" should not be interpreted as being in any way equated to some simplistic delineation between "good" and "evil," for a number of reasons.

The first is that the Greeks were far more sophisticated than to make such a distinction of deities with whom they felt they interacted on a fairly frequent basis: if individual people are rarely all good or all evil, why should gods be any different? (The concept of a god as being the "best of everything," some sort of superlative human, is not a Greek one).

Secondly, the Greek gods were not moral agents – they were neither bound by human morals nor were they particularly interested in whether humans felt bound by them, either. Certainly, some of the gods were interested in particular mortals (often as not, as mates, whether willing or no), or in human families. And certain crimes were likely to annoy some of the gods (especially ignoring the proper sacrifices, or crimes against family). But for the most part, the gods let humans get on with things and didn't get all that concerned about them – and certainly don't appear to have worried about fitting in with moral codes. (And, when you think about it, it is a pretty conceit to think that our ways of understanding how things "should be done" might apply to those who are more than human....).

Finally, the Greeks didn't make that kind of dark-bad (sinister, illicit), light/good (licit, allowed) bifurcation of either their gods or, come to that, their own magic. Yes, there are sacrifices to chthonic gods, which are rather different from those to the "Olympians" – the chthonic ones tended to take place at night, to involve rather more blood, black or dark sacrificial animals, and often the entire animal was offered to the god as a burnt offering (holocaust) rather than merely the thigh and a bit of fat (as per "Olympian" sacrifices). What is absent, however, is a sense that there was something wrong, or furtive about such offerings – they were merely for a different purpose. There are curse tablets (which are fairly "dark" by modern standards) addressed to a very wide range of deities, indeed – not merely the "dark" ones.

Nor was magic (with or without its attendant and modern "k") something seen as "dark" or menacing in and of itself. Yes, magic tended to be seen as something that was rather exotic and slightly foreign (hence Mithras' typical "Persian" cap and the idea that witches come from Thessaly[4]); but ordinary citizens were very likely indeed to carry amulets, carry out rites, invoke and sacrifice for their own ends as well as for the ends of simple worship. So although Hekate was renowned for her use of magic, this alone would not have made her a "dark" god.

Hekate's powers over the earth, which are said to be wide-ranging, have to do almost entirely with inhabited earth (men, fish, animals, cf. the young dogs presented to her at crossroads) rather than with grain, which was the province of Demeter – yet one would expect the cultivation of grain to be important to a chthonic deity, "the corn comes from the dead," after all – any society dependent on cultivation realises the importance of what is in and under the earth . This merely highlights the fine differentiations made by the Greeks in relation to their own relationships with the divine.

But she is also presented as almost a saviour of humanity. Hesiod (the earliest to mention her at any length) places her in counterpoint to Prometheus, whose works are responsible for our separation from the gods. Propitiation of Hekate, however, can bring us some measure of comfort here in our "earth-bound" existence. She is involved directly and intimately in human lives, in general presented as being benevolent but certainly capable of punishment and withholding favour as well as granting it.

This involvement continues when she takes women who have been transformed into animals as her familiars or companions: Galinthias, Gale and Hekabe become a weasel, pole cat and black dog, respectively, serving Hekate.

Her connection to the dark and the night is unquestionably ancient. And her association with the dead, that is, with those who are dead, ghosts, is well also well attested; Virgil's journey into the underworld begins with a sacrifice to her. But perhaps we owe most of our view of Hekate as the mistress of magic and witchcraft to Ovid, who depicts her as just as willing to hunt humans as beasts, as the discoverer of poisons (including aconite), and as demanding human sacrifice. Truly a dark, brooding goddess...but (and here, I suspect, we find the reason for the interest in her) one of great power, and able to dispense that power to her devotees, even as the *Theogony* maintains.

Yet we are still left with a chant that has an incongruous part to it, "let us be reborn". There is little, if anything, in the ancient conception of or cult to Hekate that leads to any suggestion of rebirth or resurrection – in general, the Greek dead stay dead. (Indeed, the differentiation between the gods and the dead is one of the very marked aspects of Greek religion). While it's possible that the mystery cults offered some measure of hope for rebirth in some form, these were the exception rather than the rule. Does such an imposition matter, though?

While the Greeks might not have understood the concept of rebirth in this way, we certainly do, and it makes sense to the modern mind to connect death and rebirth (in a way that might not have made sense to the Greeks, particularly those not involved in mystery cults).

Do we do damage to the lore, to the myth of Hekate, the goddess of the crossroads, when we impress upon it (or, perhaps, upon her) modern ideas such as rebirth from death, or "the triple goddess"? (There are indeed depictions of Hekate as having three faces or indeed three bodies – but these are not in the mode of maiden, mother and crone – though one might be forgiven for not realising that, reading some texts and websites).

Yes, if we represent our interpretations as valid for the originators of the lore: if we present Athenian views of Hekate as being maiden, mother and crone, we are certainly playing fast and free with the sources; the same holds true if we interpret her actions in favour of humanity in the *Theogony* as somehow being of the same ilk as those who would raise the dead to life (an action which after all earned Zeus' rather great displeasure when Asclepius attempted it).

If we say, rather, that this is what this goddess represents *to us*, that seems to me to be a very different matter. Yes, it is a change from the "original," but then Euripides' portrayal of the goddess is certainly different from some of what preceded it, yet we accept his work as source material (or at least, I have done so in this article). It would seem that views of the divine change and grow (one is tempted to add "mature," but that seems to court the charge of hubris – who are we to say that we understand the gods better now than our forebears?). If we take what we know of Hekate from the lore – that she is powerful and defended as such by the ruler of the gods; that she is associated with the night, the dark; with magic, witchcraft and black dogs – and add that to our current conceptions of life (in this case, the conception in the song that death is not the end of life), surely we merely continue the process which had been going on for centuries by the time Euripides picked up his pen?

---

1 Does it matter, moreover, what Hekate might make of it? Or how she and Cerridwen feel being so yoked together? This question, while important, is not the focus of this particular article, being better served by other means...

2 I see no need to use the diminutive term, "goddess" – yes, Hekate is female but she's still a god.

3 This may point to yet another connection with Hermes, for it is the messenger god who gives Odysseus the herb (mole) that allows the adventurer to resist the magic of Kirke

4 Yes, this *is* why Gaiman's witch is called Thessaly in *The Sandman* – we are told, after all, that this is not her real name.

Ashes for Hekate

by Amanda Sioux Blake

Pieces of a life
Ashes of a home
On the breeze
Soot floats away
Tiny curls of nothing
Easily crushed underfoot
Penelope's at the loom
Shredding apart the burial shroud
Under cover of nights gloom
What some would call destruction
Is really an act of creation
As she faithfully awaits Odysseus

As life never springs from a void
Creation must come from destruction
Life come from death
Change is invariably born in moments of pain
Most fear change, and treat Death with disdain

Hekate,
Fearsome Goddess,
Let me never be one to cower in my home
As your hounds bray across the night
Let me forsake the fear that binds my heart
And ride out to meet you at the crossroads
And embrace whatever comes
Lady of Ghosts
Let me meet death
With a smile on my lips
And a song in my heart

Heliotrope Hedgerow

by Christa A. Bergerson

shall we now enter the thorny thicket
the floor of the woods so fully clothed
wicked roses strangling pale picket
      how neatly the grass seems to be mowed
behind the heliotrope hedgerow lives
Hekate, a lady who surely knows
the vision of Hermes Trismegistus
and emerald tablets that ghost grass grows
follow her to the other side of time
visit the man with the thousand faces
better hurry to be the first in line
pray that you will be in his good graces
      take the key and cross through the clover door
transcend sublunary forevermore

Queen of Darkness, Heaven and Earth

by Frederick Villa

I wear the shadows
The night in my veins
I roam as I please
The keys in my hand
All show me reverence
All cross my path
The cross roads, the torches, all who are born
I am the counsel
By whom decisions are told
I rule the seas, the skies and the earth
Yet the death lands are where I call home
I am the granter of magic
The queen of the ghosts
Necromancers invoke me
With witches I'm home
Black dog and polecat
My faithful companions
With them at my side
I rule my dominions
Blind to nothing
All I know
By my graces all mortals
Good fortune shall know
Goddess and titan
That is my blood
All paths I have taken
All roads I have trod

To Hekate Trimorphis

by Lykeia

Hekate I sing of thee, night crowned Trimorphis at the gate,
Night loving, night dwelling, triple crowned are you.
O thunderous-eyed goddess, red-hooded, red-veiled,
Black is your gown in the underground, you a vein of light,
Black gowned of the deepest sea, black of the darkest night.

Phosphoros, a heavenly queen, girt in your immortal shine,
A torch burning so bright, in the nocturnal grasp of night.
The stars yield to your yew in their heavenly course,
Mapping out the seasons for the famer's seed and knife,
Good guide of weather-worn sailors on their oceanic route.
And on your star girded throne you draw the temptress night,
Hiding well the lover's embrace hand-maiden of Aphrodite.

To the light the oceans and river sing, moist-limbed Hekate,
They rush and draw about you as a lover would caress,
A stir of life resounds within its waves and watery breast.
The fish of the sea, and the aquatic beasts, do increase,
Within the net, or revoked, proud fisherman's blessed gain.
You walk upon the water, kissing upon with your silver light,
And there upon the beach you lay, to Khrysorrhapis' delight.

Companion of Oiopolos, to the fruitful beasts of men you attend,
Khthonie you arise among the flocks, young arrive to your embrace,
Sweet lullaby of life over the fields, earth's tender loving song.
And the caverns shake and open wide before your descending path,
Within your domain lays the riches and wealth treasured by man,
But to your ghostly-armed embrace, rushes the long dead race,
The spirited deceased to you come, o divine bright-coiffed Aidonaia.

Calling Across the Nights Invocation

by Pax / Geoffrey Stewart

Thrice Great Hecate, I call unto you,
Most honored amongst the gods,
Lady of the Earth and Sky and Sea,
Under brightest moon I call across the nights to you,
In the midst of darkest night I call out unto you,
Underneath the sunlit skies I call out to you,
The New Moon's Mistress,
Torch bearing, Lady of the Hounds, hear me,
You who is The Queen of Phantoms,
The Place Where Three Roads Meet,
Keeper of the Keys of Creation,
Crossroads Golden Clad Guide,
Guardian of the Gates,
Gorgo, Mormo, Thousand Faced Night,
Come unto us oh Savior,
Come unto us oh Eldest of the Gods,
Who is also the Night Wandering Maiden,
Come unto us,
Attendant of Persephone and Demeter,
Come unto us,
Bless the incense,
Come unto us,
Bless us with your presence!

Daughter of the Night

by Bettina Theissen

They call you noctis filia, daughter of the night,
and indeed in darkness you're at home.
Yet into darkness you are bearing light
and your torch illuminates the way.

They call you Trioditis, Lady of the crossroad,
and on crossroads we do often meet.
Yet not on roads of stone and grass you're found
but in the twisted alleys of our lives.

They call you Kleidouchos who bears the three worlds' keys
and you do reign in heaven, earth and sea.
Yet most important: you're the one who sees
into all hidden secrets, dark and light.

I call you, Hecate, from soul and heart,
Trioditis, key-bearer, daughter of the night,
that your dark wisdom onto me impart
and with your torch illuminate my path.

Lady of Hounds

by Amanda Sioux Blake

Hekate, Lady of Hounds
Dark-haired haunter of the crossroads
Threshold-crosser, Boundary-walker
Protect my home from all evil influences
From those who would wish me harm
And those who would harm me unwittingly
Dark-haired Goddess clad in spidersilk
The wolf and the hound at Your side
The dark of the moon belongs to You
Hekate Triformus
Keeper of Keys and Walker of Ways
Let me partake of the secrets of the night
Let me speak with the animals at Your side
And share in Your khthonic wisdom
Let me return home to sleep in my bed once more,
To teach others of You, fierce Goddess
Let me be of Your world,
Yet remain in mine.

Devoted to One of the Lady's Hounds

by Bronwen Forbes

"A baying of hounds was heard through the half-light: the goddess was coming, Hecate." – Virgil, *Aeneid* 6.257

Once upon a time there was a little beagle who didn't trust people very much and had never been loved for who she truly was. One day a Goddess stepped in and taught her and her owner how to live happily ever after. This is our story.

My love of beagles started when I adopted Herman from a local no-kill animal rescue in 2001. Herman was a red and white beagle/Parson Russell terrier mix who was my once-in-a-lifetime canine soulmate. I am a devotee of Herne; Herman was my god-touched avatar – a living representative of my hunting god in a dog's body. He was my television-watching companion on the couch after supper and slept with me "spoons-fashion" in bed at night. I bought him for my husband – something I am still kidded about; Herman was all mine and I was all his and it was obvious to everyone five minutes after I brought him home.

Five years after I adopted him, Herman was diagnosed with a genetic disorder that prevented him from digesting protein. In three weeks the doggy half of my heart was gone – I held him in my arms while the vet gently completed what a midnight heart attack (or possibly a massive stroke) started. I honestly did not know how I was going to go on without Herman. I've had – and lost – other dogs in my life. I miss them and grieved at their passing, but none of their deaths affected me as much as Herman's.

In my grief and pain I panicked, and did the worst possible thing a responsible dog person could do – ten days after Herman died I brought Bridey home. Bridey's job was to fill that Herman-size hole in my soul and keep me connected to my God. Of course she failed. Miserably.

Unlike my rescue mutt, Bridey actually has a pedigree. Her father has won championship titles from more countries than any other beagle in history, and Bridey even had a short show career of her own. Bridey also has a mild case of Musladin-Lueke Syndrome, also called Chinese Beagle Syndrome, which is very similar to Down's Syndrome in humans, complete with a slightly lower than average cognitive ability. The discovery of this "defect" is what ended her show career.

Unfortunately, because she was on the dog show circuit with different handlers the first two years of her life, Bridey had no chance to bond to her humans, or even learn how to express basic affection toward "her" people. When we went to pick her up, she was living in a home with twelve other show beagles. The dogs were either in crates in the home at night or kenneled outside in the back yard during the day. There was absolutely no one-on-one play time or cuddle time between Bridey and her former owner (an owner, I should add, who drank several rum and Cokes while we were there). This may not be normal for all show dogs, but it was for mine.

In short, the only thing she had in common with Herman was beagle ancestry.

For about six months, I tried to turn Bridey into a spiritually connected avatar, like Herman had been. I tried to get her to cuddle with me on the couch. She'd get up and move away. I tried to let her sleep with me, but since she (like the majority of show dogs) wasn't reliably housebroken, I got tired of cleaning up messes on my bedroom floor in the middle of the night and gave up.

I even knew at the time that I was trying to turn one dog into another, and I couldn't stop myself. And when Bridey didn't miraculously morph into an emotional clone of my soulmate dog, I did the absolute worst thing I could do.

I gave up on her.

Oh, I still fed her and took her to the vet for shots, but I stopped caring — which probably reinforced Bridey's pattern of not reaching out to people because she could sense they didn't love her. There were times when she'd escape from our fenced-in yard and, even as I was chasing her down, part of me was hoping that this time she'd be lost forever so I could get a dog that gave a damn about me. Ugly, but true.

My husband would look at me and say, "You were ripped off," and I'd agree with him. I was stuck with this lump of a dog that I didn't particularly care for. I even seriously considered giving Bridey back to her previous owner – the one with twelve other dogs and a fondness for massive amounts of alcohol in the afternoon.

This went on for about a year and a half.

One day after my husband said "no" to another dog for the millionth time, I decided to give Bridey another try, to give our relationship another chance. There was a bit of "I guess I'm stuck with her so I might as well try to make the best of it" in my decision which, again, I am not proud of.

So instead of resenting the fact that she did nothing to make me happy, I started to think of ways to make *Bridey* happy. Who knows, maybe it would work. We started a routine of nightly walks. I'd had a couple years to refine her housetraining skills, so I let her sleep with me again. We worked together on basic obedience commands. I bought her cow hooves to chew on (our other dogs get sick if they chew rawhide).

Finally, I decided to take her with me to a small, dog-friendly local Pagan gathering, sponsored and organized by a group dedicated to the Greek Gods – Hekate, primarily. Funny, it had never occurred to me to take a dog to a Pagan gathering before, but I decided that this might just be what our relationship needed: weekend in the woods where we'd be (literally) attached to each other every minute, and some shared ritual experience where I could ask for divine help in trying to get through to my dog.

The first night changed our lives forever.

The organizers had planned an oracular ritual, and we were given a choice between speaking (briefly) with someone who was divinely possessed by Persephone, Hermes, or Hekate. Ignorant of Hekate's connection with dogs, I couldn't decide which deity to go to.

Bridey chose for me. This twenty-pound dog literally dragged me straight to the veiled priestess dressed in black. I whispered to her attendant, "Hekate?" and the attendant nodded. I knelt before the Lady, next to Bridey, and was wiping away tears before I even spoke.

I said, "There is no connection between our hearts," and gestured to the two of us. "I want a connection."

There was silence for a moment. Then Hekate said, "I love dogs. And this one loves you, but she does not trust. I will help you heal her, and help her trust you." I thanked her, and moved aside for the next person. I went back to the picnic shelter near the field, held my dog, and cried.

Later on in the weekend, Lisa, the priestess who had worn the mantle of Hekate, spoke with me at some length. Not only had she been petitioning her Goddess on my behalf, she'd been observing Bridey and I with the eyes of an experienced dog person. "She watches you all the time," Lisa said.

"She does?" I'd never noticed.

"And when you handed her off to someone so you could make a sandwich, she was very upset."

"She was?" This is a dog that I'd have sworn didn't care if I lived or died. It's not like she even once got off the couch to greet me at the door when I came home.

What Lisa had gotten from Hekate after the oracular rite was that Bridey's intelligence wasn't the problem; being passed around from handler to handler, traveling from show to show, and having little if any one-on-one quality time with " her" person was the problem. Some show dogs thrive on all the "go, go, go." Mine shut down emotionally and it took a Goddess to point it out to me. Just as I had to teach my show dog how to sit on cue (show dogs are deliberately taught not to sit, because to sit at the wrong time in the show ring can disqualify them) and pee outside, I also needed to teach her how to trust me.

I was so ashamed when I heard that; I hadn't done such a good job of that last item over the past two years.

I wish I could say that Bridey and I were fully bonded by the time the gathering was over, but I can't. We're closer to it now, but we've got a way to go yet. She greets me at the door when I come home; sometimes she even wags her tail. She sits with me in the big comfy chair while I watch television, and snores on my bed when I'm on the bedroom computer.

I did not see what I was doing to my dog until Hekate and her priestess pointed it out to me. I love Bridey now, and I wouldn't give her up for anything. She is not my soulmate, nor is she a living avatar of my chosen deity. But thanks to Hekate's intervention, Bridey has the most honorable and sacred duty any dog can have, and she performs it well: she is my companion.

Hekate is not my patron Goddess, but She seems to continue to have a vested interest in my little beagle. I am honored to have the opportunity to care for one of the Lady's hounds.

Lady of the Hounds

by Diotima

Lady of the hounds
    Hekate
Lady of the moon
    The dark
        The dead
Lady of magic
    And witches
        And poison
High honoured lady
    Attended by hounds

Hekate of the crossroads
    Guard my coming and going
    Guard my myth and my magic
Lady of the hounds
    Guard my night and my dying.

(*Originally published in* Dancing God)

Hekate's Bitch: Hecuba and Other Greek Traditions of Cynanthropy

by Phillip A. Bernhardt-House, Ph.D.

Ancient Greek tradition has given the rest of the world the term "lycanthropy," which is to say, the phenomenon of humans turning into wolves.[1] There are a number of stories of lycanthropy in ancient Greek and Roman sources,[2] often associated with the region of Arkadia and Mt. Lykaion, with the gods Apollon Lykeios or Zeus Lykeios, and with the legendary characters King Lykaion,[3] as well as Apollon himself[4] and his mother Leto.[5] However, an analogous type of therioanthropy (human-animal transformation) occurs in the form of cynanthropy, or human-dog transformation. The two "conditions" were linked in a medical treatise of the second century by Marcellus of Side, who considered them synonymous, and prescribed very gentle treatment to those afflicted with this form of madness.[6] However, myth is not so limited when it comes to considering the possibility of human-canid transformation, and is nowhere near as reticent to have this occur in absence of scientific and metaphysical etiologies (like madness, demonic possession or illusion, etc.) for how it can occur.

The existence of cynanthropy, however, in Greek texts is far less frequent than lycanthropy. There are a limited number of instances in which Apollon was said to have transformed into a puppy to pursue the daughter of Antenor, the result of which was the birth of Telmissos and the city and people of that name;[7] and there is also a similar but very minor incident from Lycophron's *Alexandra* and the glosses on Vergil's *Aeneid* by Servius which indicate that the river god Crimissus also assumed a canine (or ursine) form to pursue Segesta (or Egesta), the Trojan daughter of Phaenodamas, who in exile on Sicily encountered the river god and duly bore Acestes (Aegestus, Egestus), for whom Egesta in Sicily was named.[8] And, in Aristophanes' *Frogs*, Xanthias reports to Dionysos that the spectral Empusa assumes many forms, among them that of a dog.[9] The majority of cynanthropic traditions in Greek and Roman literature, however, are essentially limited to two primary examples, both of which have some relation to the goddess Hekate.[10] The first is the story of Hekabe (or, in the Latin version of her name, Hecuba), the wife of King Priam of Troy, who was said to have been turned into a dog after the death of the last of her children. The second is the so-called "Wife of Ephesus" tale, known only in one fragment from Kallimakhos. These two sets of tales will be

46

examined here, but before doing so, it would be worth looking at some of the further canine associations of the goddess Hekate.[11]

The epiphany of the goddess Hekate is often associated with dogs in a number of Greek sources, including the poetry of Theocritus (*Pharmaceutriae*)[12] and Apollonius of Rhodes' *Argonautika* (3.1040, 1216-1218).[13] Lukian of Samosata's *Philopseudes* provides two particularly rich examples of this, with Hekate appearing in one instance with gigantic hounds the size of elephants and appearing as a gigantic, gorgon-like figure herself but being unable to assail the witness to her epiphany because of his possession of a magic ring in one instance,[14] and another appearance from beneath the earth with Cerberus, which included her changing shape from woman to ox, and then puppy,[15] the latter a noteworthy instance of divine cynanthropy in itself. She is also associated with canine or cynocephalic (dog-headed) forms in a number of the spell formulae from the *Greek Magical Papyri*, often in a tricephalic form with one human head, one goat or cow, and one hound.[16] The chthonic associations of Hekate and her own hounds (as well as other better-known hounds of that type, e.g. Cerberus) seems to be present in her appearances in the late second-century C.E. *Chaldean Oracles*,[17] including the implication that she is the driver of dogs of the air, earth, and water,[18] which fits with her Hesiodic praises as having dominion over those realms.[19] Hekate is also called "divine friend of hounds" in Nonnos' *Dionysiaca* (3.74-75),[20] and in the *Orphic Hymn* dedicated to her, she is also praised as hound-loving, and is connected to the three realms.[21] Hekate's persistent general association with dogs, particularly with chthonic dogs, and with both cynanthropy in herself and cynocephalic forms, therefore, makes it all the more appropriate that the two complexes of Greek cynanthropic myths to be dealt with here are intimately connected to her.

It has been suggested by Walter Burkert that Hekabe (the Greek form of the name more commonly recognized in its Latin form, Hecuba) is related to the goddess Hekate simply due to a similarity in their names.[22] However, almost from her first literary appearance in Homer's *Iliad*, her role as wife of Priam and queen of Troy, brought low in grief and disaster after the ruin of her city, is established firmly; but the particularities of her later development as a cynanthropic figure seems to be foreshadowed as well. In part of her lament speech before the body of Hector is recovered in book 24, she says, "In this way for him did restless Fate spin with her thread at his birth, when I myself bore him, that he should glut swift-footed dogs far from his parents, in the power of a violent man, in whose inmost heart I wish I could fix my teeth and feed on it; then might deeds of requital be done for my son…" (24.209-214).[23] This bloodthirsty wish for vengeance, expressed in canid terms after speaking of her son being devoured by hounds, is realized literally in a number of later Greek and Latin literary works, the most famous of which is Euripides' play, *Hekabe*.[24] The tragedy consists of the queen's fortunes after the end of the Trojan War, in which she learns that her son Polydorus, Priam's youngest son who was sent to live with King Polymestor for his protection, was killed by his host; she avenges herself upon Polymestor by tricking him, blinding him, and killing his own children with the assistance of serving-maids, who are said to be like hounds. In the end, it is prophesied by Polymestor that she would turn into a hound herself for her inhumanity, then fall from a mast-head, and her grave, the Cynossema, would forever after be a mark for navigation by sailors.[25] Further fragments of Euripides seem to attest to this same story, including one which says "Dog you shall be, pet of bright Hekate,"[26] which occurs in Plutarch's *On Isis and Osiris* 379 E.[27] A further fragment of Aristophanes likewise connects the two, saying that Hekabe becomes a dog by the statue of Hekate Phosphoros.[28]

Further, Lycophron's *Alexandra* 1174–1178, has a prophecy of Cassandra about her mother Hekabe, which runs as follows:

> Oh mother, O unhappy mother! thy fame, too, shall not be unknown, but the maiden daughter of Perseus, Triform Brimo [i.e. Hekate], shall make thee her attendant, terrifying with thy baying in the night all mortals who worship not with torches the images of the Zerynthian queen of Strymon [i.e. Hekate], appeasing the goddess of Pherae with sacrifice. And the island spur of Pachynus shall hold thine awful cenotaph, piled by the hands of thy master, prompted in dreams when thou hast gotten the rites of death in front of the streams of Helorus. He shall pour on the shore offerings for thee, unhappy one, fearing the anger of the three-necked goddess [i.e. Hekate], for that he shall hurl the first stone at thy stoning and begin the dark sacrifice to Hades.[29]

This particular tradition differs slightly, with Odysseus building a cairn for Hekabe in Sicily, after having stoned her to death; however, the status of Hekabe as canid attendant of Hekate still remains. In Ovid's *Metamorphoses*, there is a brief allusion to the story in XIII.404–407,[30] followed by the full tale of Hecuba as known from Euripides (with insertions from other sources and a few side stories), with her final canine transformation taking place at XIII.533–575.[31] Two short poems in the *Greek Anthology* allude to Hecuba,[32] with the second one (by Lucilius) critiquing the painter Diodorus on his work, making it seem as if the poet's child that was the subject of the painting has been portrayed as cynocephalic like Anubis, and that the child's mother therefore seems to have been Hecuba.[33] Hyginus' *Fabulae* 111 follows the same pattern as many of the previous tales, with Hecuba throwing herself into the sea near the Hellespont and being turned into a dog while the slave of Ulysses.[34] In Quintus of Smyrna's *Fall of Troy* 14.347-351, Hecuba is turned from a human to a dog after the death of her daughter Polyxena, and then into stone;[35] this passage is presaged by an extended simile in 14.280-288, in which Hekabe's lamenting is compared to a bitch who has lost her whelps.[36] A fragment of Nicander of Colophon's *Heteroeumena* tells the tale somewhat differently, with Hekabe leaping into the sea when she saw her home city in flames and heard her husband dying, and he specifies that that she took the form of a Hyrcanian (or Molossian) hound in doing so.[37] Cicero's *Tusculan Disputations* 3.26.63 also states that Hecuba's sorrow caused her to change into a dog.[38] Servius' *Commentary* 3.6 says that as Hecuba saw Polydorus' body, she was transformed into canine form in her sorrow, as she had wanted to throw herself into the sea.[39] The difference, however, between most of these post-Euripidean literary traditions and the Greek tragedy is that, instead of being transformed into canine form due to her bestial revenge, Hekabe/Hecuba is transformed due to her sorrow and hound-like wailing.[40]

The story is also presumably known to a variety of other ancient writers, who mention the existence of her tomb/monument, the Cynossema near the Hellespont, without elaborating much upon it. These writers include Diodorus Siculus,[41] Strabo,[42] Pomponius Mela,[43] and Pliny.[44] A strange passage in *De Dea Syria* §40 (attributed to Lukian of Samosata) also indicates that a statue of Hekabe was enshrined in the temple in Hierapolis.[45] Hecuba is remembered well into the medieval period, in CB16 of the *Carmina Burana* manuscript (which was made into the second song of Carl Orff's musical setting of *Carmina Burana*, "Fortuna Plango Vulnera"), and in Dante's *Inferno* 30.13-20, with the latter featuring her canine transformation.

In many respects, our final tale, that of the "Wife of Ephesus," is far simpler, as it only occurs in one source – a fragment attributed to Kallimakhos – and yet the implications for it are far more complex than the Hekabe/Hecuba story. The fragment is from Kallimakhos' *Hypomnemata*, and details how a king called Ephesus (a ruler of that city) had in his house a woman who offended the goddess Artemis by refusing her hospitality and expelling her from the house; in anger, Artemis changed the woman into a bitch, but then felt pity for her and returned her to human form. The woman was ashamed and hung herself with her girdle, but Artemis removed her own finery and adorned the woman's corpse, naming her Hekate.[46] This compares to a tale in which the tyrant Pythagoras of Ephesus killed the Basilids, but allowed one girl to be spared, though she was confined to a temple; she hung herself to escape starvation, after which plague and famine struck the city, and the Delphic Oracle suggested erecting a temple and burying the dead. Fontenrose suggests that perhaps we are to understand that Artemis was in the form of the girl in this case.[47] This story fits several of the details, including the location, of the "Wife of Ephesus" tale. However, the story also compares quite closely to the change of name for Iphigenia, a maiden who in the pre-Trojan War period was sacrificed to Artemis, into Hekate under Artemis' favor. The latter story, in terms of the specifics of the name change and the goddess who brings it about, also must be considered in juxtaposition with the "Wife of Ephesus" tale.[48] Are we to assume that the woman became the goddess, or merely an attendant for Artemis with the goddess' name? It is difficult to say whether or not there is more significance to this story from Kallimakhos than what our single fragment indicates, but it is another intriguing occurrence of Hekate in relation to cynanthropy.

To conclude, there is a persistent chthonic association with dogs in many cultures, including Greece, Rome, and Egypt, with monstrous hounds or cynocephalic creatures often serving a psychopomp function. As Hekate does have a likewise perennial connection with the earth, with the dead, and with pathways, it is also no surprise that a canine association has developed with her, both in terms of ordinary hounds' reaction to her approach, the presence of monstrous chthonic hounds in her entourage, and traditions of both cynocephalic forms as well as being involved with cynanthropic transformations in herself and others. In both the cases of the "Wife of Ephesus" and Hekabe/Hecuba, sorrow and suicide play into the picture greatly.

As a possible suggestion for interpretation of this, based perhaps on later philosophical traditions, Hekate (and her alternate form, Physis) are often connected to leading particular daemonic dogs in the *Chaldean Oracles*, as mentioned previously. These are earth-bound, non-transcendent creatures, an encounter with which is not generally sought after, and which in fact might impede the progress of a would-be theurgic practitioner. Becoming mired in the physical through excessive sorrow, and then rejecting life and the physical through suicide, may in fact doom someone to become such a spectral hound. Dogs are universally ambivalent, both man's best friend as well as potentially the lurking "wolf at the door" at all times, great allies in hunting and guarding and even in warfare, and yet also nuisances in their incessant barking and howling and potential to carry diseases. Likewise, Hekate is a benevolent and beneficial goddess in many circumstances, particularly for the likes of theurgic practitioners and for those who interpret her along the lines which Hesiod did; but she can equally be baneful and dangerous, even to otherwise unsuspecting individuals. An ambivalent goddess, an ambivalent creature, and an

50

ambivalence to life and physicality may in fact all add up to the expected conclusion of canid transformation in association with the goddess' influence, therefore.

Greek and Latin literatures generally provide a rather negative view of human animal metamorphoses, no matter how fascinated they seem with it, and it would not be until much later in European literature that positive manifestations of lycanthropy and cynanthropy would become possible in narrative literature. But, for the present, we can marvel at the ways in which canid symbolism in relation to Hekate is deployed in myriad ways, signifying deep-seated fears as well as fascinations with the limits and boundaries of what it means to be human, animal, or divine.

---

[1] General accounts of Greek lycanthropy include Montague Summers, *The Werewolf* (London: Kegan Paul, Trench, Trubner, & Co., Ltd., 1933), pp. 133-177; Richard Preston Eckels, *Greek Wolf-Lore* (Philadelphia: 1937), pp. 33; Walter Burkert, *Homo Necans: The Anthropology of Ancient Greek Sacrificial Ritual and Myth*, trans. Peter Bing (Berkeley: University of California Press, 1983), pp. 83-93; Richard Buxton, "Wolves and Werewolves in Greek, Thought," in Jan Bremmer (ed.), *Interpretations of Greek Mythology* (London: Routledge, 1987), pp. 60-79; Philippe Borgeaud, *The Cult of Pan in Ancient Greece*, trans. Kathleen Atlass and James Redfield (Chicago: University of Chicago Press, 1988), pp. 23-44; Daniel E. Gershenson, *Apollo the Wolf-God*, Journal of Indo-European Studies Monographs 8 (McClean, VA: Institute for the Study of Man, 1991), pp. 98-106.

[2] Including accounts in Herodotus of the Neuri, a people who were said to transform into wolves on one day a year, in 4.105; Robin Waterfield (trans.), Herodotus: The Histories (Oxford: Oxford University Press, 1998), p. 270. This is also repeated in Pomponius Mela's *De Chorographia* 2.14: Charles Frick (ed.), *Pomponius Mela, De Chorographia* (Leipzig: B. G. Teubner, 1880), p. 31, translated in F. E. Romer, *Pomponius Mela's Description of the World* (Ann Arbor: University of Michigan Press, 1998), p. 72; and also in Caius Julius Solinus' *De Mirabilibus Mundi*, Cap. 16: see http://www.thelatinlibrary.com/solinus2.html#XVI. Furthermore, in many Greek and Roman sources, the witch Circe is said to have transformed some of Odysseus' men (or their predecessors) into wolves: these include Homer's *Odyssey* 10.210-219; Strabo's *Geography* 6.1.5 (which gives the identity of the figure in the Pausanias passage noted below); Vergil's *Aeneid* 7.10-20; Pseudo-Apollodorus' *Bibliotheke* (Epitome) 7.14-16; Athenaeus *Depinosophistae* 1.10; Pausanias' *Description of Greece* 6.6.7-11; Boethius' *Consolation of*

Philosophy 4.3.17; and Augustine's *De Civitate Dei* 18.17-18. This is only a small selection of possible examples from Greek and Latin literature.

³ The earliest of these is from Plato's *Republic* 8.565d; see John M. Cooper (ed./trans.), *Plato, Complete Works* (Indianapolis: Hackett Publishing Company, 1997), pp. 1176. Further extant Greek references include Lycophron's *Alexandra* 480-481: A. W. Mair and G. R. Mair (eds./trans.), *Callimachus, Hymns and Epigrams, Lycophron, Aratus* (Cambridge: Harvard University Press, 1955), pp. 360-361; (Pseudo-) Eratosthenes' *Katasterismoi* 8: Theony Condos, *Star Myths of the Greeks and Romans: A Sourcebook, Containing The Constellations of Pseudo-Eratosthenes and the Poetic Astronomy of Hyginus* (Grand Rapids, MI: Phanes Press, 1997), p. 55; Pausanias' *Description of Greece* 8.2.1-6: W. H. S. Jones (ed./trans.), *Pausanias, Description of Greece*, Vol. 3 (Cambridge: Harvard University Press, 1933), pp. 350-353. Latin references include Ovid's *Metamorphoses* 1.163-243: Frank Justus Miller (ed./trans.), *Ovid, Metamorphoses, Books I-VIII*, revised by G. P. Goold (Cambridge: Harvard University Press, 1977), pp. 12-19; Hyginus' *Poetic Astronomy* 2.4: Condos, *Star Myths*, p. 56; Hyginus' *Fabulae* 176: Herbert Jennings Rose (ed.), *Hygini Fabulae* (Lugduni Batavorum: A. W. Sijthoff, 1934), p. 123; Pliny's *Historia Naturalis* 8.34: H. Rackham (ed./trans.), *Pliny: Natural History* (Cambridge: Harvard University Press, 1940), Vol. 3, pp. 58-61; and the Christian Augustine of Hippo's *De Civitate Dei* 18.17: Eva Matthews Sanford and William McAllen Green (ed./trans.), *Augustine: The City of God Against the Pagans*, Vol. 5 (Cambridge: Harvard University Press, 1965), pp. 420-421. The tradition of Lykaon continues into the medieval period, with John Gower's *Confessio Amantis* 7.3355-3386.

⁴ Servius' *Commentary on Vergil* 4.377: George Thilo and Herman Hagen (eds.), *Servii Grammatici qui feruntur In Vergilii Carmina Commentarii* (Leipzig and Berlin: B. G. Teubner, 1923), Vol. 1, pp. 531-532.

⁵ Homer's *Iliad* 4.101 ("Apollo, the wolf-born god"): A. T. Murray (ed./trans.), *Homer, Iliad Books 1-12*, revised by William F. Wyatt (Cambridge: Harvard University Press, 1999), pp. 170-171; Aristotle's *History of Animals* 6.35: A. L. Peck (ed./trans.), *Aristotle, X, History of Animals Books 4-6* (Cambridge: Harvard University Press, 1970), pp. 342-345; Antigonus of Carystus' *Historion Paradoxon Synagoge* 61: Anthony Westermann (ed.), *Paradoxographi Graeci* (Amsterdam: Adolf M. Hakkert, 1963), p. 77; Aelian's *De Natura Animalium* 10.26: A. F. Scholfield (ed./trans.), *Aelian, On the Characteristics of Animals*, 3 Vol. (Cambridge: Harvard University Press, 1959), pp. 320-321; and Thomas Gaisford (ed.), *Etymologicon Magnum* (Amsterdam: Adolf M. Hakkert, 1967), p. 680, lines 21-34.

⁶ Daniel Ogden, *Magic, Witchcraft, and Ghosts in the Greek and Roman Worlds: A Sourcebook* (Oxford and New York: Oxford University Press, 2002), pp. 177-178 §142. In relation to Marcellus' writings on cynanthropy and the subsequent discussion of Hecuba, see also W. H.

Roscher, "Das von der 'Kynanthropie' handelnde Fragment des Marcellus von Side," *Abhandlungen der philologisch-historischen Classe der Königlich Sächsischen Gesellschaft der Wissenschaften* 17 (1897), No. 3.

7 Dionysius of Chalcis fragment 4: Charles Müller (ed.), *Fragmenta Historicorum Graecorum* Vol. 4 (Paris: Ambrosio Firmin Didot, 1868), p. 394.

8 Lycophron *Alexandra* 961-964: Mair and Mair, pp. 400-401; Servius *Commentary on Vergil* 1.550; Thilo and Hagen Vol. 1, p. 169. See also Saara Lilja, *Dogs in Ancient Greek Poetry* (Helsinki: Societas Scientiarum Fennica, 1976), p. 103.

9 Jeffrey Henderson (ed./trans.), *Aristophanes: Frogs, Assemblywomen, Wealth* (Cambridge: Harvard University Press, 2002), pp. 64-65. Another case of serial shapeshifting, which includes a canid form, would be the Hellenistic/Ptolemaic Papyrus Jumilhac, which includes a sequence in which (after Isis has spied upon Set in the form of Hathor) Set pursues Isis, and both assume animal forms, with Set as a bull and Isis assuming the form of a dog with a knife on the end of its tail; see Susan Tower Hollis, *The Ancient Egyptian "Tale of the Two Brothers": A Mythological, Religious, Literary, and Historico-Political Study*, Second Edition (Oakville, CT: Bannerstone Press/The David Brown Book Company, 2008), pp. 197-198.

10 Indeed, Empusae were connected to Hekate, and thus the previous example given also relates to this pattern. See Lilja, p. 80.

11 For a good general account of the goddess, and the many associations she has with dogs, see Robert Von Rudloff, *Hekate in Ancient Greek Religion* (Victoria, B.C.: Horned Owl Publishing, 1999), *passim.*

12 George Luck (ed./trans.), *Arcana Mundi: Magic and the Occult in the Greek and Roman Worlds* (Baltimore and London: The Johns Hopkins University Press, 1985), p. 68; Lilja, p. 92.

13 E. V. Rieu (trans.), *Apollonius of Rhodes, The Voyage of Argo* (London and New York: Penguin, 1971), pp. 136, 141; Lilja, p. 101.

14 Odgen, *Magic, Witchcraft*, pp. 272-273 §275; *In Search of the Sorcerer's Apprentice: The Traditional Tales of Lucian's Lover of Lies* (Swansea: The Classical Press of Wales, 2007), pp. 54-55 §22-24.

15 Odgen, *Magic, Witchcraft*, pp. 254-256 §244; *In Search of the Sorcerer's Apprentice*, pp. 50-51 §13-15.

16 Hans Dieter Betz (ed./trans.), *The Greek Magical Papyri in Translation including the Demotic Spells, Volume One: Texts*, Second Edition, with an updated bibliography (Chicago: University of Chicago Press, 1992; paperback edition 1996), pp. 65 (the goddess is addressed as "O Black Bitch"), 75 (cow and dog heads), 92 (goat and dog heads); further, Brimo (often taken as a by-name of Hekate) is described as a "dog in maiden shape," as well as "wolf-formed" and "dog-shaped," in a spell on pp. 78-79.

[17] Sarah Iles Johnston, *Hekate Soteira: A Study of Hekate's Roles in the Chaldean Oracles and Related Literature* (Atlanta: Scholars Press, 1990), pp. 134-142.

[18] Ruth Majercik, *The Chaldean Oracles: Text, Translation, and Commentary* (Leiden: E. J. Brill, 1989), pp. 84-85 §91, and commentary, pp. 176-177.

[19] Glenn W. Most (trans.), *Hesiod, Theogony, Works and Days, Testimonia* (Cambridge: Harvard University Press, 2006), pp. 36-39.

[20] W. H. D. Rouse (trans.), *Nonnos, Dionysiaca, Books I-XV* (Cambridge: Harvard University Press, 1984), pp. 104-107.

[21] A. Tsolomitis (ed.), *Orphikoi Hymnoi* (Samos: University of the Aegean, 2001), p. 2.

[22] Walter Burkert, *Greek Religion*, trans. John Raffan (Cambridge: Harvard University Press, 1985), p. 65.

[23] A. T. Murray (ed./trans.), *Homer, Iliad Books 13-24*, revised by William F. Wyatt (Cambridge: Harvard University Press, 1999), pp. 578-579. A choral lyric fragment quoted by Dio Chrysostom has Hekabe made into a "fiery-eyed bitch" by the Erinyes: Theodor Bergk (ed.), *Poeta Lyrici Graeci*, Vol. 3 (Leipzig: B. G. Teubner, 1882), pp. 720-721 §101; translated in Judith Mossman, *Wild Justice: A Study of Euripides' Hecuba* (Oxford: Oxford University Press, 1995), p. 35.

[24] For an excellent commentary on this play, see Mossman, particularly pp. 35-36, 194-202, 214-217, which discuss the cynanthropic aspects and legacy of this character. See also Ra'anana Meridor, "Hecuba's Revenge: Some Observations on Euripides' *Hecuba*," *American Journal of Philology* 99 (1978), pp. 28-35; Anne Pippin Burnett, "Hekabe the Dog," *Arethusa* 23.2 (Spring 1994), pp. 151-164; Lilja, pp. 64-66.

[25] David Kovacs, *Euripides, Children of Heracles, Hippolytus, Andromache, Hecuba* (Cambridge: Harvard University Press, 2005), pp. 400-519; for Polymestor's prophecy, see pp. 512-515, lines 1259-1273.

[26] Christopher Collard and Martin Cropp, *Euripides, Fragments, Aegeus-Meleager* (Cambridge: Harvard University Press, 2008), pp. 72-73 §62h.

[27] Frank Cole Babbitt (trans.), *Plutarch, Moralia, Volume V* (Cambridge: Harvard University Press, 1936, reprint 2003), pp. 164-165. Mossman, p. 35, debates Burkert's identification of this fragment as relevant to Hekabe, but Von Rudloff, p. 56 and elsewhere, as well as many other commentators, accept the relevance of this fragment to Hekabe. See also Deborah Lyons, *Gender and Immortality: Heroines in Ancient Greek Myth and Cult* (Princeton: Princeton University Press, 1997), pp. 154-155.

[28] Jeffrey Henderson (ed./trans.), *Aristophanes, Fragments* (Cambridge: Harvard University Press, 2008), pp. 416-417 §608.

[29] Mair and Mair, pp. 416-419. For commentary, see Lilja, pp. 102-103.

[30] Frank Justus Miller (ed./trans.), *Ovid, Metamorphoses Books IX-XV*, revised by G. P. Goold (Cambridge: Harvard University Press, 1984), pp. 256-257.

[31] *Ibid.*, pp. 266-269.

[32] W. R. Paton, *The Greek Anthology, Books XIII-XVI* (Cambridge: Harvard University Press, 1918), pp. 40-41 (XIV, §27).

[33] W. R. Paton, *The Greek Anthology, Books X-XII* (Cambridge: Harvard University Press, 1918), pp. 172-173 (XI, §212); Lilja, p. 122.

[34] Rose, p. 81.

[35] A. S. Way (trans.), *Quintus Smyrnaeus, The Fall of Troy* (Cambridge: Harvard University Press, 1913), pp. 590-591. Lactantius' commentary on Ovid says fundamentally the same thing: Hugo Magnus (ed.), *P. Ovidi Nasonis Metamorphoseon Libri XV, Lactanti Placidi qui dicitur Narrationes Fabularum Ovidianarum* (Berlin: Weidmann, 1914), pp. 700-701.

[36] Way, pp. 586-587.

[37] A. S. F. Gow and A. F. Scholfield (eds./trans.), *Nicander, The Poems and Poetical Fragments* (Cambridge: Cambridge University Press, 1953), pp. 144-145 §62; Lilja, p. 104.

[38] J. E. King (trans.), *Cicero, XVIII, Tusculan Disputations* (Cambridge: Harvard University Press, 1927), pp. 300-301.

[39] Thilo and Hagen, Vol. 1, p. 335.

[40] Mossman, pp. 214-216.

[41] Diodorus Siculus' *Library of History* 13.40.6: C. H. Oldfather, *Diodorus Siculus, Library of History, Books 12.41-13* (Cambridge: Harvard University Press, 1950), pp. 230-231.

[42] Strabo's *Geography*, 7 fragment 55: Horace Leonard Jones (trans.), *Strabo, Geography III, Books 6-7* (Cambridge: Harvard University Press, 1924), pp. 376-77; and 14.2.14: Horace Leonard Jones (trans.), *Strabo, Geography VI, Books 13-14* (Cambridge: Harvard University Press, 1929) pp. 280-281.

[43] Pomponius Mela's *De Chorographia* 2.2.26: Frick, p. 34.

[44] Pliny's *Historia Naturalis* 4.11.49: H. Rackham (trans.), *Pliny, Natural History, Books 3-7* (Cambridge: Harvard University Press, 1942), pp. 154-155. See also Jennifer Larson, *Greek Heroine Cults* (Madison: University of Wisconsin Press, 1995), pp. 21 and 165n76, for alternate traditions of Hekabe's death and the location of her tomb (mostly in scholiae on Lycophron).

[45] Harold W. Attridge and Robert A. Oden (eds./trans.), *The Syrian Goddess (De Dea Syria) Attributed to Lucian* (Missoula: Scholars Press, 1976), pp. 48-49.

[46] Rudolf Pfeiffer, *Callimachus, Volumen 1: Fragmenta* (Oxford: Oxford University Press, 1949), pp. 352 §461.

[47] Joseph Fontenrose, *The Delphic Oracle, Its Responses and Operations, with a Catalogue of Responses* (Berkeley: University of California Press, 1978), pp. 76-77.

[48] Larson, pp. 153-154; Sarah Iles Johnston, *The Restless Dead: Encounters Between the Living and the Dead in Ancient Greece* (Berkeley: University of California Press, 1999), pp. 242-246.

Hekate Devotion

by Marian Dalton

I am the sound of midnight in an empty house
I am the frozen silence of the grave
I am the mistletoe that strangles the oak
I am the cessation of breath and the slowing of the heart
I am blood-let and life-stop
I am white as bone, red as blood, black as earth
I am the end of every quest
I am the closing of the eyes
I am the crossing of the hands
I am the coin upon the tongue
I am the *memento mori*
Inescapable

Dark Moon Light

by Christa Bergerson

Go now conjurers
deep in the land of bones and stones
where wailing willows walk
betwixt the roads
fern grass grows ghost petals
trees wear faces in their cloaks

Follow the twisted cypress
down the meandering path
listen – when hounds howl
she will rise, wax
luminescent
a will–o'-the-wisp
lantern beckoning
shades wandering through woods
where incantations flow
from the babbling babbling brook

Prayer to Hecate

by Holly Cross

Hecate, goddess of blinding light
goddess of illumination, show me the way.

Hecate, goddess of the crossroads
goddess of protection, bless my path.

Hecate, goddess of the baying hounds
goddess of fear, allow me to conquer.

Hecate, goddess of the sky, earth and sea
goddess of the three realms, teach me about nature.

Hecate, goddess of the three heads
goddess of the Arts, grant me the power of sight.

Hecate, goddess of menstrual blood
goddess of women, bestow upon me, your power.

Hecate, goddess of women's magic
goddess of the craft, lend power to my workings.

Hecate, goddess of ancient witches
goddess of the old ways, help me keep the mysteries.

Hecate, goddess of blazing torches
goddess of the lost, deliver me to safety.

Hecate, goddess of Circe and Medea
goddess of sisterhood, be a mother and sister to me.

Hecate, goddess of night and darkness
goddess of the midnight sky, wrap me in secrecy.

Hecate, goddess of the black butterfly
goddess of change, transform me.

Hecate, goddess of shimmering keys
goddess of knowledge, open the world to me.

Invocation to Hekate

by E. A. Kaufman

Hekate of the Three Ways, I invoke You,
Maiden of the Land, the Underworld & the Seas as well,
Chthonia, Enodia, Phosphoros,
Propylaia, Atropaios, Propolos,
Kourotrophos,
Adorned in saffron robes, shining in the Night,
Nocturnal One, Keeper of the Keys, Lady of Torches,

Hekate, hear me.
Upon this night, the way is open,
Be with me at the Crossroads of the Worlds.
You who are Keeper the Mysteries,
You who lead me to journey across the River,
You who are the Pale Mother,
Be present at this my Hallowed Rite.

I bow to You, Lady.
With scent & flame I make offerings to You.
With honey & cider I pour a libation to You.
I have given my blood that You may know me,
Keep me.

For I am one of Your Especial Breed.
I bow before You, Hekate,
Come, Hear me, Know my Name,
Be with Me.

Saffron Robed

by Diotima

Bright coiffed Hekate
>Mistress of magic
Mistress
>Of the dead
Saffron robed
>Highly honoured
Cross roads call you
Lady of the ways

(*Originally published in* Dancing God)

Dancing Hands

by Holly Cross

Magic from afar
starts with magic close at hand.
Sister Hecate sways
as she grinds the herbs beneath the pestle.
Her long, slender fingers of white
work quickly, gliding
through the steps of the spell.

With one drop of rain, herbs of the earth
 and salt from the sea, she pours herself
into the bowl, impregnating the preparation
with power.

She spins to face the distance
and sees the destination in her mind:
a man on a horse, dressed in armor.
She scoops the compound into her palms
drinks in the wind
and blows the words across her dancing hands.

The soldier sees a comet coming for him
and then he falls to the cleansing earth.
The horse bolts, leaving her master behind.
His message of war will never arrive.
His cold heart was stopped by the dart of a Queen.

Hekate's Offering

by E. A. Kaufman

I am the darkness,
Waiting, silent in stygian stillness.
I am the silent stillness,
Waiting, full, ripe with knowing, bliss.
I am the amorphous knowing,
Waiting, bringing truth, healing.
From Beneath, within the rich, redolent Earth,
I wait.
From beneath, within the crystal, renewing waters,
I wait.
From above, within the winds that whisper and take,
I wait.
The darkness holds and heals.
The water blesses and heals.
The wind cleanses and heals
These are my offerings. Will you accept them?
Here is my torch, I hold it for you,
Opening the path.
Light within darkness.
Here from beyond.
Wisdom from knowledge.
As you have offered to me time and again,
Blood and honeyed wine, herb and egg,
Garlic and almond, fig and date,
Now, I offer to you.
From the three realms I come
To the crossroads where you have called to me.
Will you join me there?
Will you journey with me
To my caverns of darkness and light, soft and still,
Mother's embrace?
Will you accept my gifts: visions, dreams,
Let your spirit fill and flow?
Will you come, O priestess of Hekate,
priestess of mine?
Come, be with me, I am waiting.

Windsong

by Bettina Theissen

I can see you
in the darkness
ahead of me.
The light of your torch
is barely enough to illuminate
the distance between us.
Somehow
I stopped once again on my path
and now you are waiting,
waiting for me to resume my rightful place
at your side.
I hurry up.

Serving Her

I've been serving Hecate for a long time. Over those years, I've worshipped her in different ways, for a multitude of reasons. One of the most touching and intense ways I have served her is as *psychopomp*, as a person who helps conduct the souls of the dead to their resting place. I take this particular role very seriously, and have engaged in it since prior to learning about Hellenism.

My lessons as a working *psychopomp* began when my maternal grandfather fell gravely ill. He suffered a massive, fatal stroke, and was kept on life support only long enough for me to travel home (I lived some 2000 miles away at the time) to say goodbye. I arrived late in the day and rushed to the hospital, where nurses told me that he would be removed from life support and would likely die within the hour. The family gathered around his bedside, to be with him and to provide one another with comfort during our time of grief.

He did not die.

His body struggled on, unwilling to pass. He had always been a strong man, vital and in control, and his passing was difficult. The family decided that an airway would be left in, in order that he should not suffocate to death (an option none of us found acceptable), but that no other measures would be taken. We were assured he was basically dead already, but that it might end up being several days before he finally let go and died.

I felt him, that night. He hovered close, and it felt as if he were waiting for something. After a long discussion, I convinced my family to leave me at the hospital, and to take my grieving grandmother home and care for her and see that she got some sleep. The nurses provided me with a cot so that I could sleep in the little room they'd provided for him as a courtesy. I sat in the chair beside him and talked.

Instinctively, I had felt that I needed to say words and prayers to help him move on. I had known that before I ever walked into the room, but when I entered, it was even more obvious. I had brought along a copy of the Egyptian *Book of the Dead*, not knowing what else to use, and I began to read. I told him about his grandchild, about my life, and when his breathing calmed and became quiet, I told him that my grandmother was at home in the arms of the family, and that it was alright to go. I told him we loved him, and that it was his time, and that I would be with him.

I sat there for hours, holding his hand into the night. I stayed there until his last breath came out of his body. I stayed there until his skin cooled to my touch, and I felt his essence was gone. It was a powerful moment for me, and I was surprised. I did not feel grief; I felt joy! I was sad that he was gone, yes, but the fact that I was there with him at the end made me feel a sense of quiet calm, of welling love for this man who had loved me unconditionally.

I was proud to stand as minister at his funeral, and it was my first official act as a minister. It has touched my ministry in many ways. It is my belief that Hecate saw something in me as a child, and later as an adult, and that she picked me because I have the capacity to deal with death without the uncontrollable grief most others experience. It isn't that I don't grieve at all – I do, very much so. Even those who I didn't know well, such as a boyfriend's father who died while I was present, elicit feelings of grief. But for me, it is not a crippling thing, but something freeing.

In my time as a pagan, and later as a Hellenic polytheist, I have dealt with several deaths. Some of them have been far away, and I have been called on to bring comfort and aid the grieving process for those left behind. Others I have attended personally, standing by as I did with my grandfather. I take my responsibilities as Hecate's priestess very seriously, and try to convey that seriousness to others. I find that people turn to me in grief, almost instinctually, and often the right words come to my mouth without my seeking them. They are just there, when I need them. When those moments come, I do my best to be a vessel, to stand and let the light of my goddess pass through me, to give succor and balm to those who hurt.

Hecate is a goddess of many things. She's an enigma, a mystery. Her prominent place in the Eleusinian Mysteries has confused scholars through the ages. I've found that it's better to simply accept what Hecate sends my way, to roll with the punches, so to speak. Struggling against the tasks she sets me to seems to only make my life unnecessarily difficult. Her mysteries are vast and innumerable, and I'm proud to plumb them in the various ways that I do.

On the Modern Worship and Understanding of Hekate

by Lykeia

When taking into consideration the majority of general pagans out there who worships Hekate, it is disturbing to see how many align Hekate within a very narrow function: Hekate is granted Queenship of the Underworld. The temptation is there, of course, to ask what happened to Persephone, but that will generally be met with a firm belief that Hekate ruled the Underworld before Persephone – regardless of the fact that evidence indicates that she was not a true underworld goddess.

In the rape of Persephone, Hekate was not located within the underworld, but rather within her cave. A cave is a mediation point between the worlds of the living and dead; and therefore associated with many chthonic pastoral gods (think: cave of Pan). It was from this vantage point that Hekate was a witness. Other than declaring herself as Persephone's handmaiden later in the *Homeric Hymn to Demeter*, and with Hermes' aid guiding the goddess back to the world of living, Hekate doesn't have a lot of direct influence over the underworld. Another example would be her function in the Aeneid where she had to be drawn from her caves that lay at the passage into the underworld so that Aeneas could slip past and within. More commonly she is associated with ghosts instead, and is seldom mentioned as literally being in the underworld other than in reference to the Hekate's lunar light traveling to the underworld and the moon absent from the sky.

Rather than an underworld goddess Hekate is more likely a goddess of transition between life and death. Her deipnon, or feast, was offered not in either traditional chthonic or celestial practices. Neither buried nor burned, but rather left out in a manner appropriate to a goddess between the worlds, and offered at the crossroads where the spirits lurk. At birth Hekate is there, and at death Hekate is there. There must be a reason why dead women accompany the goddess. Why wouldn't they if she were leading them to their place of rest. They are spoken of very generically in a manner that would suggest that it is not the same group of women accompanying her everywhere, unlike Artemis and her specific nymphs and hounds. It is unlikely to be a permanent thing, but rather as she wanders the night she draws the souls of dead to her train. She doesn't rule over the Underworld but she is queen over those earthbound ghosts that exist between the worlds, even as she leads others into the next world. Those who died violently before their own time was up, much as Hecuba is in her company, the grieving wife of Priam whom Hekate took in the form of a night black dog. But even these angry spirits are unlikely to stay with her forever.

Even dogs themselves are connected to both the land of the living and that of the dead. Friend of men, the baying hounds of Hekate and Artemis, and the guarding Kerberos. Dogs are very much a part of our living lives, unlike dragons which have a history associated with chthonic goddesses such as Gaia and Demeter. The fact that dogs were offered in sacrifice to Hekate says much about this. Hekate has been linked to the whelping bitch as a fertility symbol bearing her litter of pups, who nurses and nurtures. This is highly represented of her nature in presiding over fertility, as much as goats (who get a bad rap for their later associations with Satanism). Hekate appears as both, and received sacrifices of both. That the fertile earth gives way to death and life renews again.

However the crossroads seems to be the most well known component in Hekate worship. And why wouldn't it be since the crossroad goddess looking in three ways is very popular in Hekatean art. Though it does seem to be stressed primarily as the spot where Hekate lurks more than anything else, for one would leave feasts to the goddess at these crossroads. These feasts were given to the goddess in preparation and purification for the coming of the new month. By the very nature of the feast belonging neither wholly to a heavenly god nor the chthonic gods below, it invited the hungry poor to feast at her plate. Whether this was viewed as acceptable can be debated, but there were those who took advantage of the goddess's feast. With this in mind, there is a grisly fascination with the crossroad goddess and her feast as it inspires the imagination of wandering spirits, snarling hounds, and the goddess with the serpentine hair wandering on her darkest night.

Still this image persists, accompanied by her control of sorcery. When you get right down to it Hekate is not really depicted as a sorceress. However as a goddess that illuminates the hidden it would be common knowledge for her. She is presented more frequently in teaching the arts to those who are favored by her. As a goddess of the sea she can whisper about the powers of the sea that can be harnessed. As a goddess of the earth she can whisper of the growing things that can be gathered and used. In her connection with the moon she can tell of how to ensnare the moon, and as such and her starry heavenly realm she guides the course of good days for planting, gathering and this guide can be equally useful in sorcery. So while she aids and instructs the sorceress, it is more in her revealing and all knowing capacity rather than as a literal goddess of sorcery. Though despite this there is no denying that she does preside over the magical and mystical.

Overall there is little support for the doom and gloom Hekate that is valued by so many as a terrible goddess. Yes she is an awesome goddess, with a primal power that will invoke fear into those who are not familiar with her. Primal is the best description for her as it illustrates her nature as being one of wilderness and natural laws. The raw power of a Titaness connected intimately with the natural world. We depend on her to eat, whether in gathering fish or having fruitful herds for these things are within her hands. Fertility, life, and death. The sexual urge to mate and reproduce. The mother to nurture from her own flesh. In these things she shares her world with Hermes who, like her, assists the dead back to their final abode, masters the herds, and travels between the worlds. He is also one who shares in the chthonic snakes, goats and barking dogs.

She exists outside of civilization even as she is at our roads and homes. And there she exists walking all roads of the earth, below, and between us and the gods. Civilization cannot exist without the consent of the wilderness. The Latins claimed Diana as goddess of civilization even as the Romans recognized the contribution of Silvanus. Hekate straddles both worlds: civilization, and wilderness, as she straddles the worlds of the living and the dead. Probably not such a far stretch in associations considering that forests were considered dangerous places filled with predators.

But what, then, of the night? Isn't the night under her domain and associated with death and danger? True, she is associated with the night, but as the nocturnal light. The bright light of the full moon sheds enough light to see comfortably by, enough so that particularly bright moons are called Hunters' Moons. She illuminates without dispelling the darkness. Even her governing of the starry heavens is governing of the brilliance of light sparkling. She does not dispel the dark for it is in the night that she shields the lovers embrace, and in this fashion has been called the Handmaiden of Aphrodite; for Hekate can conceal even as she reveals. She is both the brilliant light and dark blanket of night.

This is the nature of Hekate, one that is both simple and complex and the same time, often contradicting; and one that needs to be taken into more account by the general pagan populace of those who worship and serve her.

Hekate

by Hearthstone

Hekate, wise one, walker in the dark
who moves swiftly along hidden pathways.
In bright flames in the night, uncertain roads
made clear, in shifting lucent visions,
in hard choices made, in shadows embraced,
in all these are you well known, Hekate.
Hekate, knower of things unknown,
seer of things unseen, guide of the lost,
guardian of spirits, friend of the helpless,
we thank you for comfort and for shelter,
for a despairing heart's flutter of hope.
O Hekate, we praise and honor you.

Oblation

Hecate, I offer you the honey of the swarming bees.
Hecate, I offer you fish, fresh from the sea that is yours.
Hecate, I offer you eggs, whole with the promise of new life.

Hecate, I offer you blood, red as the birth blood that marks your hands.
Hecate, I offer you flowing water from which all life springs forth.
Hecate, I offer you wine, sweet and fit for a goddess.

Hecate, I offer you meat, just as the followers of old did.
Hecate, I offer you almonds, leached of their poison.
Hecate, I offer you olives from the trees of your homeland.

Hecate, I offer you cakes and ale to share with you.
Hecate, I offer you cheese, made from the milk of goats.
Hecate, I offer you fresh figs, the sacred fruit of the lands to the east.

Hecate, I offer you mint, the herb of many names.
Hecate, I offer you garlic, the herb of magic and medicine.
Hecate, I offer you aconite the herb of moth food and witch potions.

Hecate, I offer you the black poppies of night and sleep.
Hecate, I offer you the yew berries of death and rebirth.
Hecate, I offer you saffron, the plant of endless uses.

Hecate, I offer you my ruddy feet to walk your path.
Hecate, I offer you my henna-stained hands to do your work.
Hecate, I offer you my dancing like the women of the temples once did.

And all these things, Hecate, I offer you me.

My Journey With Hekate

by Krysta S. Roy

I have been devoted to the Hellenic deities for over a decade now, but it was just about 3 years ago that I encountered Hekate for the first time. Up until then, I hadn't heard much about her, and what I had heard was mostly misinformation: she was "evil," she was "scary," she's an old crone who spawns "demons," she'll feed you to Cerberus if you so much as look at her the wrong way. I knew better than to believe everything I heard, especially from the sources it was coming from, but nonetheless, Hekate was still a goddess I felt very wary of for a long time. And as I was preoccupied with Athene and Apollon at the time, I really didn't give it too much thought.

And then I fell on particularly rough times, a real "dark night of the soul." I was alone, bleeding and broken, or at least that's how I felt. I spent most of my time fighting back tears during the day at work, letting the floodgates open when I got home. My anxiety was at an all-time high, and I felt almost paralyzed. I was just going through the motions of life and not really living. I didn't sleep much, but when I finally passed out from sheer exhaustion, that was when the dreams began.

What struck me most about these dreams was that they were so very vivid. Almost three years later, I can still remember exactly how everything looked, felt and sounded, even though most dreams fly away from my memory almost as soon as I wake. At first I didn't know where the dreams were coming from, I just took notice because they were so powerfully memorable. I dreamt of a spider spinning a web in a tree whose trunk split into three main branches. I dreamt of a black dog on top of a hill howling at the crescent moon like a wolf. I dreamt of floating keys finding their way into locks that were invisible until the moonlight shone upon them.

After several weeks of these dreams repeating, then came the "grand finale." All the different dream images from before seemed to blend into one. I was on my bed in the dream. The tree with the spider and her web was to one side, the dog on the hill was to the other. The bed was set in the middle of a crossroads, with one road behind me and two roads stretching out in front of me. A snake coiled and struck me, biting me on the arm. The full moon was overhead and a woman who looked about my own age suddenly stood in front of me, wearing indigo robes and a key tied to her waist, holding two torches. I guess if you know her well, the neon signs would have been flashing long ago,

71

but at the time, I didn't realize it until all the symbols came together in this dream.

The woman came up to my bed and set her two torches into my bedposts and gave me a look that I can only describe as pity mixed with exasperation. "You were meant to do more than this," she said in almost a sigh. "You had dreams, you had goals and now you're frozen in place like a statue." She reached her hands out to me. "It's still your choice. Will you let this beat you? Will you let those who aren't even worth your time keep you down? Or will you trust me — trust in yourself — and rise up?"

I took her hands and she pulled me to my feet. Then she said, "Fear is not a weakness in itself, but courage is moving forward through it, moving forward despite it. If you are willing to move forward, then I will be beside you." The two roads ahead began to glow around the edges, and stars began to appear in the sky around the moon. And as soon as I took the first step, I woke up. I grabbed my journal and wrote everything down just in case the dream faded, though as it turns out, it hasn't faded at all. Nor have I ever had a repeat dream visitation like it.

After I got out of bed and went about my day, I started doing some research. Though I had an inkling after the two torches in the dream, a friend confirmed my hunch and suggested I start researching Hekate. I ordered a few books and did a lot of web research in the meantime. And while I would say that she's definitely a goddess that won't put up with any BS, she's also not quite the "scary goddess" I had originally been led to believe she was.

It was through researching Hekate that I came upon the religion I now practice, Hellenismos. I also found out about Hekate's deipnon and started doing a ritual to honor her each month. While the vivid dreams have not made a reappearance, I find Hekate's guidance comes particularly strong through divination, and the readings I do after addressing my questions to her directly always seem to be easier to understand, and I'm able to know just how they apply to my specific circumstances.

She's the goddess of the crossroads, and it's fitting that she came to me at a time when my own life was at a crossroads. I credit her with helping me heal and regain my strength, helping me pick up the pieces of my life and make more empowering choices for my future. My instincts feel stronger and I've been learning to trust my own intuition more. I feel more guidance and inspiration than I did before, as well as a strong push to actually do something with my talents. I feel as though I'm living my life with a greater sense of meaning, able to focus more on what's truly important and to get less caught up in what's not so important.

I am so very grateful for Hekate's presence in my life and all she has done for me. I continue to honor her on a daily basis, and hope that the living of my life itself can do her honor. One thing is for sure, I am so much better off than I was before she entered my life. She continues to guide me and inspire me each and every day.

Apology to Hekate

by Jennifer Lawrence

I tell people I don't know you,
But that's really not true, is it?
Early on in my studies,
I heard a lot from those who I considered
Less intellectually rigorous than me,
About how wonderful you were,
      how powerful you were,
      how mystical you were.
Mysticism has never been an interest of mine,
Magic never something I cared to pursue.
History was what caught my attention,
And literature,
And it angered me to no end
To see those who did not even
Worship you in your proper context
Glorifying you while in the same breath
They claimed you were the very same
As Kali and the Morrigan
(And I see some similarities,
But you are not they,
And they are not you,
No matter how many people may
Believe it to be so,
Nor will it ever be, no more than
A bird is the same thing as a bat or a plane,
Simply because all three things can fly.)
So, yes, I know of you,
Although you and I have never been close,
But it is not your fault
What fools may believe of you,
So I should save my anger
For those of a fool's bent
Rather than blaming a god
For the deeds of their worshippers.
Therefore, I ask your forgiveness,
Prytania, Crataeis, triple-headed crone,
Mistress of the crossroads
And the hounds that howl at midnight.

Henceforth, no longer will I deny it
When folks ask if I know you,
And perhaps someday,
We might be more than strangers,
Two ships passing each other in the darkness.

On the Edge

by Jeremy J. Baer

You may think, dear reader, I have a moving essay for you concerning how Hekate suffused every fiber of my very soul with a transcendent joy and imminent clarity of purpose. I have no such story, however. In fact, Hekate is low on my list of divine priorities. And that is what I want to share with you, actually.

Please do not mistake me. I have no intention of besmirching or belittling a profound deity. In fact, the public defamation of a divinity – what some people call blasphemy – is against my own personal creed as well as the creed of Neos Alexandria. Rather, I wish to present a contrast to most submissions in this anthology, which presumably were written by people who consider Hekate their patron or primary deity. One does not need to be so close to the goddess to appreciate her. She can stand comfortably at the edges – and, in fact, the periphery is where she often best belongs.

Polytheism is a complex web of overlapping relations between human and divine in a great drama of life. The 'stars of the show' – the most popular deities who are usually proclaimed as patrons – can dominate the press. The supporting cast and bit actors need to be appreciated for what they are. Going back to the original point, then, Hekate is a great supporting actress and can be easily honored within the constraints of that role.

In modern Hellenic polytheism it is quite common to devote oneself to one or two deities above the rest (commonly called patron deities, though some dispute the term). Then below them there may be a few more deities whom one honors fairly regularly but not with the same intensity of a patron. Further still, beneath those there may be various deities one honors infrequently. One's choice of a particular hierarchy is defined largely by personal proclivities, though historical realities such as lunar calendar observations and yearly festivals tend to factor in as well. Hekate can and does fit quite easily into the lower scheme of things. Let us find out how.

In ancient Athens, during the last day of the lunar calendar – the dark of the moon – food offerings were made to Hekate, a meal called a deipnon. The goddess was a guide and guardian of liminal bounds, not unlike Hermes. There was often a shrine to Hekate on the doorstep of peasant homes. It was in this capacity the Athenians best knew her. She was an outsider, warding away certain unsavory elements from the inner sanctum of one's home. A literati named Hesiod had tried claiming Hekate was second only to kingly Zeus, but most Athenians would have none of it. She simply wasn't in the company of great deities who dwelt on Olympus.

We shouldn't underestimate the importance of household worship, of course, but equally we shouldn't overestimate it. The home is the most immediate social unit in someone's life. But it is not necessarily the most important. Classical Athens was a very communal society and the civic life of the city-state is where citizens directed their attentions. The Athenian citizen lived life on a very public level in the social milieu demanded by neighborhood (*demos*) and the greater city-state (*polis*). Other gods who had a role to play in household worship, like Zeus and Apollo, had internationally renowned panhellenic cult centers. Hekate did not have this.

Modern Hellenes inspired by ancient Athenian religion often afford Hekate the same monthly devotion as the ancients, on the dark of the moon. And they view her in the same capacity – a guide and guardian situated at the edge of domestic considerations.

My own view of Hekate aligns somewhere with this model. Given that the city-wide public festivals are gone (probably for good), domestic worship is the most easily reconstituted level of Hellenic religion. An offering once or month or so for guarding the proverbial or literal doorway to the home seems incumbent. Beyond this, I have no great relation to the goddess, nor feel the need for one. My higher devotions are to other divinities who more fully command my interests.

But what of the popular image of Hekate as the über-goddess of spellcraft? Later in Greek religion she did become associated with sorcery, ghosts and the underworld. This is the aspect of Hekate most consonant with neopaganism – though, strangely, neopagan devotees tend to portray the lithe, torch bearing young maiden as a Gothic crone. And despite the Gothic love of the macabre, modern imaginings tend to gloss over certain facts of her ancient cult, such as the fact that puppies were sacrificed to her. In any event, I have never been particularly interested in "witchcraft," especially when it merely serves as a convenient scheme of 'empowerment' for alternative minded individuals.

Deities demand different things of different people, but to some people a deity may neither demand much nor promise much. The guardian of the crossroads and the doorway teaches me to look at the bigger picture and recognize those blurry elements in the background we may initially gloss over. By keeping watch at the gates, I feel secure in the privacy of my domicile, and am better able to devote my deeper attentions to other things. It is here, on the edges, in a modest but respectable role, that I found the goddess.

And it is there that I leave her.

Finding Hecate Where Three Roads Meet

by Pax / Geoffrey Stewart

"Goddess of the Liminal Points, Lady of the Wilderness, Queen of Ghosts, Thousand faced Night, Mistress of Sorcery, mighty Hecate may your lanterns light shine forth in the darkness and guide my head and my voice, guide my heart, my hands, and my feet as I tread these cross-roads paths."

Hear and attend my friends, of my first meeting with Hecate, and how I didn't recognize Her at the time.

It was a bit more than a decade ago, I was newly self-dedicated to Neo-Pagan religious Witchcraft (of the kind popularly called Wicca). It was the early 90's and after a lifetime of fascination with history and mythology and the occult I had found modern Paganism and was reading voraciously and throwing myself at the gates of mystery with all the eagerness of a newly minted Pagan. I was living in downtown Anchorage, Alaska and working in Midtown. I was working the night shift and walked home along some of the bike trails near West High School and Westchester Lagoon.

A dear friend of mine had recently given me a sealed letter and told me to hold onto it for her and if "something" happened to her I was to give it to her parents. I was deeply worried, and she was short on giving me any details. It seems so melodramatic and teenage, even though we were both in our 20's, but at the time it was horribly serious. Not knowing what else to do I turned to the Gods, or rather a Goddess. At the time I felt a pull from the Celtic gods and goddesses. It *was* the early 1990's and all things Celtic were all shiny and popular.

I was walking along a bike trail after work one night at about 2am. I had been doing a lot of thinking about whom to pray for, for protection for my friend, and decided upon the Morrigan. I had also decided that I should utter this prayer at a cross-roads. I really am not sure why, it felt right at the time, what little I could find out about the Morrigan she had a cross-roads/liminality about her, at least to my mind and soul at the time.

I thought hard about my words and, as I walked home that fateful night, I approached this place where three bike trails intersected forming an imperfect "Y." I spoke my prayers to the Morrigan, prayers of protection and defense for my friend, just as I crossed the boundary from the path to the cross-roads and finished my prayer at the center of it.

Then, the Morrigan deigned to notice me…

There was an intense onrushing of Power and Presence, as deep and powerful and ancient as the ocean and its tides or the majestic mountains of my childhood. I stood there feeling as if I was being picked up and examined from every angle. Held carefully in strong yet gently cupped hands. Scrutinized to the deepest part of my head and heart and soul. Then there was a sense of...decision...and then She was gone.

I stood there, stunned and not quite sensible at that point with every last wit scared right out of me. It is one thing to believe in the Gods, it is another to be closely scrutinized by one and have their reality thrown into the depths of one's psyche. As an acquaintance of mine used to say, truly a "This shit is real!!!" experience. I stood there, stunned both by the encounter and its implications, not knowing what to do or where to go next, then She came.

There was this much lighter sense of presence. A sense of amusement, not at my expense so much as at the foibles of youth, gentle and kindly and as old and enduring as the wilderness. I heard these thoughts that were not quite/entirely my own...

"It's OK. The Gods are like that sometimes; try not to make too big a deal about this. Go home, get some sleep. Things are being taken care of as they should. It's all-right..." Not words so much but thoughts and feelings. As I stumbled home from the cross-roads the 'voice' and presence stayed with me dragging/escorting me safely home.

Now I know that that presence was Hecate...I had called to Morrigan, but Hecate is always there. She is the cross-roads, at the liminal points where decisions must be made, she even stands as Guardian of the Gates as one of the Gods of protecting the home. One of her many roles is that of guardian and guide.

At the time, I slept, and did not think much about the experience for years, scared away from exploring the Celtic pantheon especially but wary of the Ancient Gods in general. I kept to the Lady and Lord of Witchcraft and didn't muck about with any other gods for a good long time.

Life happened, and I studied my Craft and grew and learned and wandered off the spiritual path, and then back on. In that time I also moved across the country. A couple of years ago I was beginning to get involved and active in a local Pagan community group when some extremely unpleasant e-mails led me to back away from being involved with them. I was saddened and depressed by this turn of events and felt the urge to write a prayer for guidance, and following some inner urging to pray to Hecate, of all gods, I wrote the prayer that begins this piece.

After that I found myself seeking or running into information about Hecate whenever I was online. I had some realizations about my cross-roads moment, and I also offered a place in my life and heart to the Saffron Veiled Lady.

I am now, and always, a Witch; I am also a budding Hellenic Polytheist, a devotee of Hecate, a Bacchant, a citizen of Neos Alexandria, and a Seeker once more. Whatever happens and wherever I journey in this lifetime, I am really not all that worried because She is with me.

Hekate Soteira

by P. Sufenas Virius Lupus

Khaire Hekate Soteira, triple-formed,
lady of lions, mistress of hounds,
favored-one of Zeus, above all
triumphant over earth, ocean,
and vaulted heaven flecked with stars.

She is glimpsed by the dark of moon
at crossroads and on-ramps alike,
no door, no gate can obstruct her path;
horse and sail are hers to influence,
whirring engine and tail-lights at night.

With bright torch and barking dog
god and titan, nymph and satyr,
daimon and *psyche*, man and hero
have no choice but to go wherever
she has directed the crowd to surge.

The three who are one, the one who is three,
knowing virgin, ferocious mother,
animal-headed, cynanthropic,
the one who is three, the three who are one,
the voice of the formless fire, *Khaire Hekate Soteira*.

Hekate, Briefly in a Dream...

by Renee Rhodes

I was falling through space. Falling through dark, endless, lightless space when my feet suddenly touched the floor. There was still no light, no way to guide me, I couldn't see. I only knew that there was a solid floor beneath my feet, and somehow I knew that I was in a hallway – despite there being no tangible walls.

I had fallen like this several times, each time, the floor dissolving beneath my feet. This time, the floor hadn't dissolved and I considered whether to walk forward or not. Before I really had time to think, there was a presence, intangible and solid all at the same time, sinuous and serpentine, flowing around me on all sides then expanding until I was completely surrounded.

I felt pressure, a pressing into my skin from every point. It was an odd sensation, but somehow not intrusive or overwhelming. Then I had the sense of someone walking around me in circles, as if inspecting me. Eventually, I had a feeling of approval – I had passed this inspection – or whatever it was.

And once again, I was falling through space.

Long Beach, Hekate

by Todd Jackson

Under dark She rolls the waves.
She is phosphorus curled inside the wave
That has caught light off the pier's lights that shine downshore.
The waves' skin grey-black from the sea-floor's soot, and above,
Grey-black from the clouded Night. The Night-clouds that mass and
  ripple, Hers,
Not less than the phosphorus glowing, curled inside the grey-black
  waves.

Hekate at Lagina and Çatalhöyük

by Tim Ward

[Excerpted, with the author's permission, from *Savage Breast: One Man's Search for the Goddess*]

Anatolia, Turkey

O nether and nocturnal, and infernal
Goddess of the dark, grimly, silently
Munching the dead,
Night, Darkness, broad Chaos, Necessity
Hard to escape are you...: you're Moira and
Erinys, torment, Justice and Destroyer,
And you keep Kerberos in chains, with scales
Of serpents are you dark, O you with hair
Of serpents, serpent girded, who drink blood
Who bring death and destruction, and who feast
On hearts, flesh eater who devour those dead
Untimely, and you who make grief resound...

—*Papyri Graecae Magicae*, a 2nd Century A.D. Hymn to Hekate[1]

It raises the hackles on the back of my neck, this late hymn to Hekate. Can we imagine her as this poet did, in the second century after Christ, as a goddess who munches the dead? She is so clearly the vessel into which the destructive spirit of the Furies were poured. The hymn even calls her *Erinys*, the Greek word for "Furies" and describes her with serpent hair and scales. Dogs were sacred to Hekate because they ate corpses, and so Cerberus, the three-headed hound of who guards the gate to hell is under her control, as the hymn proclaims. This portrait reminds me of Kali, Hindu Goddess of Chaos who I encountered in India, who also a drinker of blood, queen of charnel-grounds, and devourer of the dead.

Yet when I began to research Hekate's origins, a startlingly different goddess appeared. Pre-classical drawings and sculptures depict Hekate as a torch-bearing maiden. She is described as "bright coiffed" in a Homeric Hymn, and "lovely" in an Orphic Hymn. In *Theogony*, Hesiod says Zeus honored her above all others. He describes her as a "noble goddess" who grants supplicants their wishes, makes journeys safe. She blesses fishing, flocks, competitions, battles and childbirth. Hesiod tells us her parents were Titans, which indicates that her cult was pre-Olympian. Yet Zeus treated Hekate better than the Titans he defeated and banished. He "did not use force on her and took away none of the rights she held under the Titans, those older gods," writes Hesiod. While other goddesses were raped or married, Hekate was singularly respected by Zeus. For 41 lines Hesiod lavishes praises on Hekate, far more than he devotes to any other goddess. You get the sense that he is trying to curry favor with her, and wants to stay on her good side.[2]

There is only one myth in which Hekate shows up as a key figure. It's the tale of the rape of Persephone. Hekate is the one who hears the girl's cries when she's being abducted, and it is she who leads Demeter to the sun god Helios who tells them what happened. Hekate appears again near the end of the story, when Demeter agrees that Persephone will go back and forth between earth and the underworld. Hekate offers to be the girl's constant companion and guide.[3] This close connection with Persephone and Demeter has led many to identify Hekate as the third phase in a fertility trinity of maiden, mother and crone. But the relationship between these goddesses is much more complex. Hekate is also called Aidonaia, or "Lady of Hades, and Perseis, after her Titan-father Perses, "The Destroyer." The root and meaning is the same as Persephone. Hekate is also identified as Brimos – the Terrifying One – the name given to Persephone at Eleusis, the goddess who gives birth in fire. What some experts make of this is that the underworld role of Hekate got mixed in with the Olympian myths, obscuring her older, pre-Greek identity.

So who was she originally? Some scholars point to Anatolia in Turkey, where her cult center was located among the Carians, and the ruins of her main temple stand today. Other scholars have called attention to the Egyptian Hekat, the mid-wife goddess whose sacred animal was the frog (because of its resemblance to a fetus). To the Greeks, Hekate was also known as Kourotrophe, Nurse of the Young. But she was also called The Three Formed – a three-headed goddess who oversaw many things with triple phases, including the moon. She dwelled in wild hilltops, moors, and desolate places, but also by roads, harbors and cemeteries, and if ever someone was out all alone, and felt suddenly afraid – that was Hekate he or she was sensing. Additionally she was guardian of doorways, crossroads, and keys. All these multiple, diverse identities confused me at first. Yet in them a common thread can be discerned: Hekate is a goddess of transitions, and a guide whose torch leads the way from one realm to another. Altars to her were set up at the doorways of houses, and also temples thresholds. They were also raised to her at crossroads, where travelers have to choose which path into the unknown they would have to take. Transitions were fraught with danger, even terror, in the ancient world: childbirth, death, meeting brigands or wild animals on the road, stepping through a temple threshold into the presence of the divine, even leaving the safety of your own home. As a goddess of change, Hekate was invoked to bestow her gift of illumination, a torch to guide one safely to the other side.

So how did a goddess so highly honored degenerate over time into the repository for all the dark and fearsome forces of the feminine divine? In truth, Hekate's destiny was the exact opposite of Athena's, who became the repository of positive forces. I suspect it was due to Hekate's unpredictable nature. You could pray to her when crossing a threshold, but not take her attention for granted. She could curse as well as she could bless. As the centuries progressed, Hekate's realm became more focused on concrete thresholds: crossways, doorways, and graveyards. She also began to be associated more exclusively with the unclean byproducts of these threshold such as rubbish (swept out over doorways) and corpses. The later Greeks made her a hideous hag and flesh-eating ghoul, her skin pallid and decaying, her robes a shroud. Jacob Rabinowitz, author of a modern treatise on Hekate, *The Rotting Goddess*, points out that her descent reveals Greek attitudes towards material existence. He writes that they yearned for the clean, heavenly air of Olympus, the purity of Pythagorean mathematics and Plato's ideal forms. Ooze and decay have no place in the life of a disembodied mind, yet the messiness of birth, sex and death refuses to disappear. It is one more version of conflict of Apollo and the Python called *Rot*.

One other attribute of Hekate became prominent in later times. She was known as Queen of the Witches. As goddess of transitions, Hekate was naturally connected with prophecy, consultation with the dead, potions, and magic. Hekate's daughters were the two most famous witches of Greek mythology: Circe (who turned Odysseus' sailors into pigs), and Medea (who used her magic to aid the hero Jason). A 3rd Century B.C. epic, *Argonautica*, describes Medea as a priestess at Hekate's temple, and goes into great detail about her magic rituals. Media was notoriously bloodthirsty. To aid her and Jason's escape from her father (from whom they stole the Golden Fleece), Medea cut up her brother and threw pieces of him into the sea. This slowed her father's pursuing ships as they stopped to collect the dismembered parts. Later she tricked the daughters of a politically troublesome king into chopping their father up and cooking him. She did it all for love of Jason. So when he jilted her for a Greek-born princess, Medea exacted her revenge by murdering her and Jason's children.

As Queen of the Witches, Hekate lived on long after the establishment of Christianity in Europe, and our fairy tale notions of witches have much in common with the later Greek characterizations of her. We all know witches are old, warty, foul, vindictive and cruel. They live in forests, on the boundary of the wild. Their pots bubble with threshold creatures like snakes and bats, frogs and newts, which they use to cook up powerful spells. Fairy tale witches may eat children, and certainly they ride Hekate's broom (the broom we still use for sweeping rubbish out the threshold). In reality, of course, the women who were accused of witchcraft were not especially foul or warty. They practiced midwifery, divination, and herbal medicine. Like Hekate, they were helpers through difficult transitions...birth, troubles, sickness, death. The Church could not tolerate the competition. Its sacraments and prayers were to be the sole guide through life's transitions. The Church killed ruthlessly to ensure its monopoly. Although the witch hunts had many social and political causes, I wonder how much of it was the obsessive theological urge to root out the last vestiges of the old order. What made it easier to demonize witches was that they could so easily be cast in Hekate's gruesome image, an image that already terrified people for centuries before the church rose to power.

If long ago we projected this fear of the Rotting Goddess onto witches, today we have only ordinary women to be the repositories of this peculiar loathing. And it is weird that this creepy feeling is only attached to old women, and not to old men. Perhaps this explains why so many men as they grow older dump their wives for younger women. To be married to a crone at the archetypal level is to consort with death. So, like old Hades, aging men seek out Persephone, the maiden, with hopes she'll make them young again. But Hekate is inside of us, inhabiting a dark corner of our anima. We can't get rid of her.

I get a flicker of something vile when I contemplate the image of the Rotting Goddess. She viscerally repels me, yet draws me, as if she holds a secret for me inside her fetid mouth, a flicker of truth about men's revulsion towards feminine flesh. I remember a friend of mine – he was only in high school at the time, and yet he understood this all so well – told me he had found an easy way to break up with a girlfriend after he no longer wanted to be with her. When they started making out, he said he would keep his eyes open, and he would just examine her, as if through a microscope. He would stare at the glistening pores, pimples, blackheads, the creases, hairs, erupting moles and folded skin. He would feel nauseated, and that would be the end of his attraction for her. In my twenties, in India and Thailand, I learned Buddhist techniques for eliminating sexual desire that followed much the same course. I was told to imagine a woman's body split up into five heaps of skin, nails, hair, teeth and internal organs, or to visualize a woman as nothing but sacks of blood and pus and shit. Feel desire for that? Thus men learn what it is to treat women like dirt (as matter, not *Mater*) and break their spell over us.

To dig up the origins of Hekate's cult – to exhume her, if you will – required going back to a time long before the Greeks, before the Minoans and Maltese Temple Builders. Back almost ten thousand years to a time when grasses had been newly tamed into wheat and barley and wild game into goats and cattle, to a time when people ceased their nomadic wanderings and began to live in villages. One such settlement on the edge of the great Anatolian Plain got conditions so right that between 7,500 and 5,500 B.C., seven thousand or so people lived stacked together at one time. Houses were built upon houses in successive generations until they formed a great mound, the only hump on a vast and marshy plain. It was an unprecedented massing of humans so astounding that the world would not see its like again until the city states of Mesopotamia, three thousand years later. This was a crucible of civilization, and in its many shrines one finds the symbols that dominated western religion throughout the ages and still echo for us today: Çatalhöyük, the first city.[4]

Teresa and I climbed to the top of the mound, wild grasses swishing at our knees, and looked at the trenches of the first excavations, made barely thirty years earlier. The finds are now in Ankara, some on display at the National Museum, a vivid window into the past. You might think they would have been a simple people, occupied with their animals, plants, basket weaving, still hunting game on the grasslands, maybe carving rudimentary totems. Take one look at the reconstructed shrine room in Ankara, and you see how wrong such a picture would be, see how fruitless it is to interpret the past by drawing a line back and down from the present.

Against the smooth plaster wall of the shrine, three bull skulls line up, floor to ceiling. The heads are covered with smooth clay, leaving the wide horns sweeping out in triplicate. Above them, sculpted right into the wall, a splay-legged woman squats. She seems part frog, part human. It appears she is giving birth to the triple bulls beneath her. My mind reels. Is Hekate here? More bull skulls jut up from the floor on columns. The shrine walls were once covered with paintings. On the walls of the museum some of these drawings have been lifted intact from Çatalhöyük, providing a vivid window to the past. There are scenes of a hunt: a massive aurochs bull, a stag, a boar surrounded by tiny black men holding spears. The human figures seem to dance and float around their prey, perhaps even leaping over it, prefiguring the bull frescos of Crete by over 4,000 years. The city itself appears on one scene, with an erupting volcano far in the background. Another panel shows the great black wings of griffin vultures, flapping around headless bodies of the dead.

James Mellaart, the British archaeologist who first excavated Çatalhöyük in 1960, believed they practiced excarnation, the removal of flesh from the bones of the dead. Vultures and other carrion eaters served this ritual purpose quite well.[5] Mellaart's team removed over three hundred skeletons from beneath the floors of excavated houses, where the picked-clean remains were buried – perhaps to keep the spirits of the ancestors close to home. One portion of a wall painting shows tall wooden towers, each with a stairway to the platform at the top. On one platform, vultures tear at a headless corpse. On another, they feast on a head without a body. The head seemed to have a special spiritual significance and served as a special offering, or as a container of power. Human skulls were found on the floors of the shrine rooms in company with the bulls, and a few (male) skeletons have been found decapitated.[6] A third wall painting shows a peculiar symbolic pattern that hints at the meaning of some of these rites: a double row of vultures face each other, their bent wingtips touching each other to form a diamond shape; and in each diamond, the body of a woman; and within each woman's belly, the dark outline of a child. The flesh-eating vultures seemed intimately connected with birth. I imagined a Çatalhöyük mother and child, watching the vultures tending to their gruesome task on the tower. The mother explains it something like this:

"You see, first the vulture eats the bodies, then the life goes back inside the mother, where it can grow again and turn into new babies."

Maybe this is how we inherited the story of the stork?

There's also evidence that goddesses or perhaps real women were sacred to these people. In a grain bin at the site, Mellaart found an eight-inch statue of a woman seated on a chair, a throne perhaps, because the sides are two standing leopards on which she rests her arms. He labeled her the Great Goddess, and it's easy to see why. She looks old, with folds across her massive belly, folds on her knees, her breasts sagging down across her sides, buttocks bulging out from the back of her seat. She seems sculpted from real life, not some abstract notion of divinity. The head was broken off at the neck, and has been restored in the museum with a mold from a female head from another statue, so one has to imagine her without this false face. She is solid, imposing, more queen than mother of fertility and the fields. The resemblance between her and the fat Goddesses of Malta is striking, though she is at least two thousand years older.

Some experts think that the round lump between her legs is a newborn child. I have seen it unambiguously labeled so in many books about the goddess. But examining the statue for myself, I don't think that's right. There's not a single mark on the lump to identify it as a baby, and the lump lies between her feet on the floor, which seems weird. Given that the rest of statue is rendered so realistically, I think the thing between her legs may be an offering instead: a hunk of meat, a loaf of bread, or perhaps a severed head. A head makes the most sense to me, in light of the skulls found scattered about the shrine room floors. (In any case, the recent excavations of Ian Hodder's team at Çatalhöyük revealed that "fat woman" female figurines are a small minority of the total, while more than half of them were animals. Naomi Hamilton, a gender archaeology specialist working on the site also noted that the "fat woman" type of statue does not appear at all until the settlement was several hundred years old, and that most figurines were found in waste areas of the site, not shrine rooms. Her implicit warning seems to be, don't over-interpret the meaning of the "Great Goddess" figurines at Çatalhöyük.)[7]

The aspect of the shrines some experts find most sinister and most disturbing are the molded shapes protruding from the walls. Identical in form to a woman's breast, some of them have red-brushed, natural-looking nipples and it looks as if they are indeed breasts. This is strange enough by itself. But other breast-shaped protrusions contain the skull of a vulture with the beak sticking out in the place of a nipple. Others contain the jaws of a jackal, or the tusks of a boar. Scholar Michael Rice writes about this in his book, *The Power of the Bull:* "Thus the Mother's breasts do not deliver life-sustaining milk but are rather the agents of death, symbolized by the animals who are her attendants. It is difficult to resist the idea that the vultures' skulls, peering out of the Goddess' breasts, suggest a profound degree of psychological disturbance experienced by the priests (if priests they were)." Rice adds that it may not be coincidence that in ancient Egypt, the word *mwt* means both mother and vulture, and that the hieroglyph for mother contains a vulture's iconic shape.[8]

Other experts, most notably archaeologist Marija Gimbutas, see in these artifacts not a gruesome death cult, but symbols of regeneration. The vulture, jackal and boar are all carrion eaters. To Gimbutas they are the goddess' special agents for churning dead bodies back into the cycle of life. Thus we have returned to Hekate's realm again. The symbolic beak-in-breast may represent the "eating back" of living things into the belly of the goddess to be born again. On the back of one of the vultures feasting on the towers, a double ax is clearly etched – the same symbol of regeneration the Minoans used four thousand years later.

I told Teresa about Gimbutas' ideas while we wandered through the Çatalhöyük museum exhibits.

"Makes perfect sense," she said. "Mother Earth gives us birth, and yet from the moment of that birth, she hungers for us to return to her again."

"It's a strange way to look at death," I said.

"Oh, women understand death better than men: they have the power to create life, and this must be balanced in them with the capacity to destroy it. Women can appreciate death as part of the cycle of life because they are at the center of it. It's harder for men. Think of it this way: Woman is the vulture. Man is the bull. She's the Divine Feeder, in both senses of the word."

"And we men are what, the meat?"

Wandering though the museum, one thing was clear to me: these people experienced death not in the abstract, but viscerally – as viscera, exposed and eaten. What would it be like to enter into their world? I imagined going down the ladder into that twilight shrine, the great bull horns curving up to the ceiling, the black vulture wings drawn across the walls. I search for that clay breast, take it in both hands and put the vulture-nipple to my lips. As I suck, I feel the beak in it tear at my tongue, the flesh of my cheeks. White milk gushes into my mouth and my red blood flows back into the beak. No way to escape the longing I have for that breast. Though it wounds me, I go to her as a child, my cannibal mother. The image flashes of the son/lover statue entwined around the larger female, and this is how I feel, bleeding into her and clinging to her. Little comfort that she eats back the living when I am the one that she's gnawing on. It's too real, this fusion of need and fear.

And yet, I have known exactly this feeling locked in sex with Teresa. At times our lovemaking draws out a consuming urge in her that she fights against. She tells me she's afraid she'll hurt me, or scare me away. I have to hold her down, make her feel my strength so that she can let loose her self control. Then her teeth begin to chatter, as if she wants to gnaw at me. She holds back with all her will. Her face turns dark, almost black. She's right. It terrifies me. But it thrills me too, to be in the presence of something so strange, so hungry. I'm fortunate to have known the ravenous goddess Kali in India. It gives me some pattern I can fit to Teresa's transformation. Without this, I would have pulled away. How many women, I wonder, must hold their ravenous inner demons back from men? But for me, finding the dark goddess in her was deeply erotic. Once when this strange urge came over her, I fed her pieces of cantaloupe with my fingers while we were having sex. She tore at the soft orange flesh gulping it down, chunk after chunk, as if she were starving, her eyes fixed wide on me. We both knew that in that instant who she really was consuming.

I have to wonder, did the men at Çatalhöyük feel anything like it when the vulture-mother swooped down on corpses, when the frog-woman gave birth to triple bulls, when they looked up at night to the horns of the waning yet regenerating moon? Was this grassy mound perhaps, during its thousand years of life, the origin of all that I feel now towards the death aspect of the goddess, stripped back to the core?

From the plains of Çatalhöyük Teresa and I drove into the Anatolian hills, a primitive, eerie landscape of dark forests, heavy clouds, small stone villages where donkeys outnumbered cars. For long stretches there's not even grazing sheep, just black-rock hillsides covered with a sheen of green. These hills were once the stronghold of the bloodthirsty goddess Cybele, whose secret rituals cured Dionysus of his madness. There's a brooding wildness about them still. When we reached the Turkish Aegean coast, all this changed. The mountains became the dazzling backdrop to a string of beaches and an azure sea. The Ionian Greeks colonized this shore after the Dorians invaded their homeland around 1,100 B.C. The Ionians fled across the Aegean, and in the centuries that followed Greek religion fused with that of the native Anatolian peoples – the Phrygians, Lycians, Lydians, Carians, and many others – so that the old Anatolian gods and goddesses often took on the names of Greek divinities, but with a darker, bloodier edge.

The first archeological site we hit was Side, an ancient Greek fishing village. Fancy restaurants, flashy jewelry shops and boutiques are crammed cheek by jowl next to the ruins. Touts called out to us and thousands of other visitors who swelled the boardwalk in German, French and Italian. It's a tourist gold rush. In vain, Turkish archaeological authorities tried to get the locals to resettle further up the coast so that proper excavations could be conducted in Side. But the villagers refused to budge. They clung like barnacles to the old stone temples, and today everybody is making a killing off the tourists. Teresa and I strolled past the cafe-lined waterfront, wandered through an Ionian temple, and peeked inside the ruins of a 6th Century Byzantine church that has been converted to a bar called "Apollo's Disco." Eventually we reached Charlie's Scandinavian Restaurant, which shares a lot with a fenced-off pile of rubble identified by a sign as the *Temple of Men*. That's "men" as in "menses," the lunar cycle, not "men" as in "males." Men was the old Anatolian moon god, the plaque explained, and the temple was built in the shape of a half moon, still discernable beneath the overgrowth and jumble of stone blocks.

Since the beginning of this search for the goddess, I had always thought of the moon as feminine, a symbol of the goddess. This was not always so. The modern scholar Joseph Campbell says that across the Near East and Arabia the moon was considered male, because in its crescent form it resembled the horns of the goddess' bull. Its waxing and waning cycle symbolized the death and resurrection of the sacrificial bull-god. Tammuz, Attis, Dionysus, Osiris all wear his horns.[9] This crescent remains a potent symbol of the divine in Turkey and all across the Middle East, cast in gold on top of every mosque. The goddess herself accompanies the lunar bull across the heavens, appearing at his side as the morning star at dawn and the evening star at night: the planet Venus. In the Near East she was called Astarte, from where we get the English word for "star." Next to the crescent horns she still appears on each Islamic country's flag. In countries where women have no vote, where they are confined in purdah, married off as property, forbidden to attend school, and may be murdered by their kin if they are raped in order to erase the stain on the family name, the goddess' star still flies as the symbol of the divine.

We traveled north along the Aegean coast, headed towards the Letoum, holy of holies of the Lycians. These were the ancient people the scholar Bachofen believed to be a matriarchal society. Driving through farmland, we eventually reached three temples in an open field. One was dedicated to Leto, their Great Goddess, whose rape by Zeus supposedly symbolized her cult being taken over by the Greeks. A second temple was dedicated to Leto's divine twins, Artemis and Apollo. A third, much older, was just a rough stone foundation. Pottery shards date it to at least 800 B.C., which would make it older than any temple in Greece. The identity of this earlier divinity is unknown, but experts suspect the temple was dedicated to the original Anatolian goddess of the Leto cult. Who was she, we wondered, as we picked our way through broken stone slabs. How could her name be forgotten?

According to Hesiod's *Theogony*, Leto's mother was the titaness Phiobe. Phiobe's other daughter, Asteria was the mother of Hekate, which would have made Artemis and Hekate cousins. While it's fanciful to trace the goddesses' family trees, it is true that Artemis and Hekate do seem intimately related. Both are associated with desolate and wild places, with midwifery, and with dogs – though for Artemis, dogs were her companions in the hunt, not the graveyard. In post-Classical times, they were both considered goddesses of the moon. Artemis governed the full phase of the moon, while Hekate governed the dark. Indeed it seems the two goddesses attracted polar opposite energies as the Christian era approached. Hekate became the Rotting Goddess, drawing to her all that is negative and terrifying, while the wild huntress daughter of Leto evolved into the benevolent Great Goddess, Artemis of Ephesus.

Teresa and I wove in and out of the mountains, through a strange schizophrenic land of concrete tourist towns and ancient mysteries: the Chimera, a hole in the earth where once upon a time, fire emerged.

Labranda, the weird mountaintop sanctuary of Zeus where girls were sacrificed on the altar of the god with a labrys; Demre, the tomb of Saint Nicholas, the original Santa Claus, with his church built on the site of a temple to Artemis; Aphrodisias, a city dedicated to the goddess of love, but fused with bloody Cybele and served by her castrated priests; and the sanctuary of Endymion, a male sleeping beauty. As the Greeks tell the tale, the moon goddess fell in love with handsome, young Endymion. She put him into a deep sleep and hid him in the hills so she could lie beside him every night. In this somnolent state he somehow fathered fifty daughters by her. His temple was a now-familiar half-circle shape, and Endymion, it seems, was just a Greek disguise for the old Anatolian moon god we discovered at Side.

We took a long detour down a dirt track to Lagina, a clearing on a slope above a fertile valley. This was the site of one of the two known temples to Hekate. The foundations of the other I had already seen at Eleusis. This one had been built by the native Carians. There was no fence at the site, no ticket booth, no venders selling postcards. Excavations had not yet started for the season, so it was completely deserted. We stopped beside the giant stone gateway to the temple, re-erected, I supposed, since every other block and stone was shaken to the foundations by an earthquake and lay about in heaps of rubble. How suitable, I thought, that the one structure resurrected so far was her threshold. The air around was warm and something prickled in it. Teresa said she felt a presence. Through the temple entranceway, a stone staircase led down to a pool, a poisonous milky green. Small water insects rose up from the opaque depths and sank back into it again. It's the kind of pool one has nightmares about, about something down there, where the staircase leads. Hekate, if she still lives, dwells at the bottom of this pool.

A Turk in a baseball cap stood up from beneath a tree, stretched, and thumbed two tickets off his pad for us. He spoke few words of English. Nimble as a cat, he led us through the ruins, pointing out markings in the Carian script and here and there the sculpted head of a lion, a floral motif. He gestured towards a twisted grey-green branch lying on the rocks, and as his shadow crossed it, it writhed and slithered down a crack. Teresa yelped. Our guide grinned. Not poisonous, he tried to reassure us. He led us to a grey stone trough, big as a bathtub. He drew an index finger across his neck to mimic a slit throat, and made as if to pour his blood into the trough. I imagined it filled with frothing red. "Of bulls," he said, making horns with his fingers on his head, "of bulls." He ended the tour at a clear stream that welled from an ancient source, Hekate's Spring. We thanked and tipped our guide, then I went back to gaze once more into the fetid green pool just past her threshold.

It was there, down deep, that revulsion I feel like an instinct that says, don't touch! Don't dip so much as a finger in that water! Something, something will wrap itself around you, pull you in and suck you down.

It's not death that makes me tremble at the water's edge. It's the moment before death, the moment at the threshold when the living consumes the not-yet-dead: the maggots, the scum, the crawling things that cover the skin, decay that is life at its most primitive. It's the knowledge that *she* is hungry for me, that I am prey to something I can't escape, and when I look into the green ghoul-eyes of her face, I feel the fear of it right through me. Not the simplicity of annihilation. That seems almost sweet by comparison. No, this is the spider that eats the living fly. That slow consumption by the septic force, dissolving and sucking, that is man's fear, the fear he senses behind every woman's smile and stockinged leg. But we don't know it. It's underneath, as if it's frozen in ice. Yet we feel the hatred that this fear arouses, hatred like a hot brand our forefathers seared into us for a hundred generations back: Eve the deceiver, responsible for our fall from grace, the one who brought us death disguised as lunch; or Pandora, the beautiful woman, designed to inflict on man every evil released from her unlucky box; Medea the witch, whose spells transform us and destroy us.

What can I do? I reached down for her, as if plunging my hand into this pool, up to the shoulder, groping in the slime. Such revulsion entwined round the feminine here, at the most reptilian layers of my brain. It makes me despair. Hekate's is the face I see on Teresa in the throes of her dark passion, the sucking jaws, the appetite for my flesh. The she-beast unleashed, gnawing on my neck. I feel her starving mouth on my body, sucking like the void. Succubus, ghoul, witch, thing of the earth, consuming my flesh – no, my immortal soul, the thing of the heavens my forefathers fashioned to escape her clutch. Woman the spider, woman the leech, woman the parasite, the maw, and this slow emptying of my vitals into her.

Why is it then, that when Hekate glimmers at me from Teresa's face, I hold her close, and long for her teeth on me? Exactly for this, exactly because she fills me with terror. My little self flees in horror. The shell disintegrates, and in its place, *I am.* The darkness arises in me, still terrified of her, but alive. Then I notice that though she is totally possessed – I believe the strength in her could rip me apart – she does not hurt me. She loves me in some strange sense. Sometimes in the midst of her rapture, I can let go of her, let her jaws fall upon me, out of control. Fear sears right through me then, as if I'm scalded by it. It is so intense, I have to surrender to it. All pretense, all identification with my ego gets burned away. I feel her consuming my soul, devouring my essence. Truly, it is a death, and I feel as if I am hanging in empty in space. No thought, no feeling, just the rawness of the void coursing through me. With my rational mind, I know this is not possible, this identification of the self with infinite space, nor the sense I have that this emptiness is alive and humming.

Teresa usually passes out at about this point. It's fortunate for me she's never punctured a major blood vessel.

Back at Lagina, Teresa touches my shoulder, softly, to bring me out of my trance, says it's time to leave. We have a long drive ahead of us, she reminds me. We're headed for Ephesus, where Artemis (Hekate's opposite, the bright side of the moon) had her great temple. I wrench my gaze from the green water, breath deep and break the spell. I realize I envy the Carians, envy them for knowing Hekate well enough to build a temple to her, for being able to spill blood and worship her terrifying nature. They retained the darkest essence of the goddess from Çatalhöyük, so many millennia back, and she still lingers in Lagina. I lean in over the pool one last time, and long to see her shadow.

---

1 *Papyri Graecae Magicae*, 4:2854–67, quoted by Jacob Rabinowitz in *The Rotting Goddess*, p.62.
2 Hesiod, lines 411–452.
3 Homeric Hymns, page 129.
4 The very first smaller agricultural settlements in the Middle East appear around 12,500 B.C. Unfortunately, these sites are in volatile regions which I could not visit.
5 Ian Hodder, who for the past 10 years has been conducting new excavations at Çatalhöyük has questioned whether excarnation was practiced as a prelude to burial, as Mellaart asserted. (See *The Goddess and the Bull* by Michael Balter, for an excellent account of the new excavations.
6 Ibid, p. 288
7 Ibid, p.113.
8 Rice, p. 77.
9 Campbell,, *The Masks of Gods*, p. 58.

The Dark Mother

by Dee Estera Fisher

I am Illumination. I am Darkness.
I am the Titaness born of Mother Night and Cosmic Ocean,
even Zeus yields to my powers
I reign over Heavens, Earth, and the Underworld.

Behold I am Hecate Triformus.
Maiden, Mother, Crone.
I am the Ruler of the Dark Moon.
I am the Keeper of the Cauldron.

I hold the keys to Life, Death, and Rebirth.
I am the Watcher of the Past, Present and Future.
I am the reborn Goddess Hecate, born of Hera and Zeus.
I am the Mysteries of Womanhood.

I am a Lover, I am Celibate.
I am the Midwife, the Mother and the Barren One
I am the Shamaness of Visions, Dreams and Nightmares.
I am the Healer. I am the bringer of Death.

I am the Protector of the weak.
I am Revenge to those of you who harm my children.
I am many things. I come to all who seek me.
You can find me at the Crossroads, where four directions meet.

To know me is to know the greatest joy and the worst sorrow.
I am Hecate.

97

Fourth of July Torchbearer

Set a small rod aflame
And the sparks begin to fly
A mere child's amusement
Becomes a portal to another time...

I see myself carrying your flame
Walking to the crossroads at night
The fire's warmth propels me
Softly murmuring your name...

The Moon is dark and hidden
But we know it's still there
And on this night we honor you
Leaving offerings in your care...

My head turns to gaze at the stars
Bright across the moonless sky
And read in them a symbol
One of many ways you guide...

The shower of sparks brings me back
Scent of sulfur fills the air
The light burns down to a single flame
And into it I stare...

As it fades into a glowing ember
I speak your name upon the air
Knowing, tinged with wonder
I can find you anywhere.

Night-Time Prayer to Hekate Antaia

by Antonella Vigliarolo

Bright-coiffed daughter of Asteria,
Keeper of all secrets of the night,
Guide to all those who are walking over the edge, in their small and great ways,
Take my heart in your open palm tonight,
Disclose the veil,
Bless my eyes so they can become Your eyes,
My soul so can burn of Your fire,
And my mind so it can grasp Your sacred omens.
Dark Queen, crowned with oak-leaves and coils of wild snakes,
Ever-knowing, All-seeing Shamaness,
Cradle my dreams in Your dark womb.
Hekate Antaia
Hekate Antaia
Hekate Antaia
I give myself over to You

Hekate Found

by Scott B. Wilson

where one road
splits in two
did I sit and wait
hidden by a tree
as twilight faded
and darkness came
the cacophony of
frogs and goatsuckers
gave way to silence
save an owl calling
in the distant wood
closer and closer
I heard the shrieks
of a woman spectral
who I did spy
hunched over with
a braying donkey's
hindquarter
mirrored by
a leg of brass
polished smooth
and bright
in its knee
did I see
my own
eye
as she
passed
If this
is but
a scout,
then how
terrible will
her Mistress be?
maybe for
another hour
did I sit without

movement or
sound
twin stars
on the horizon
burned like
embers in
the sockets
of some
steel servant
forged by
Hephaestos
to tend the
gardens of
Olympos
but these stars
grew larger
and traveled
down the road
nearer and nearer
until I realized
that they were
the flaming heads
of torches
held by unseen
hands
this must
be She
and as I thought
the words
I could hear
those horrible
hounds said
to guard Her
every step
I knew this
willow trunk
and its weeping
leaves would never
shield me from
the eyes of a Goddess
who can pierce
three worlds
at once
and so I did regret

my boldness
and awaited
my fate
but when the light
of the torches did
reach me
night was lifted
from the spot
and everything
glowed saffron
where one road
splits in two
the Queen of
sea and sky
and earth
subservient
to Zeus and
Fate alone
came into
my view
a little girl dressed
in yellow tunic
curls brushing
Her shoulders
as She hopped
barefoot among
wide-eyed puppies
black as coal
tumbling over
one another
in play and
yipping as
She encouraged
them on with
gentle kicks
for Her pale
hands held
torches
much larger
than Her arms
Is this She who
helped the Gods
themselves defeat
those primal Giants

sent by a Gaia enraged?
YES, She answered
for She was in
my head
and from that
moment on
I would never
be the same

My First Time

by Holly Cross

I sat with my legs crossed
freshly bathed and perfumed,
wearing a light, white nightgown.
There were candles all around
and an altar at my knees.
I closed my eyes and began to breathe.
I dreamed I was flying over a beach,
along the blue green waters of the Black sea.
I met a woman there, standing in the sand
the wind whipping through her hair
and a black dog pacing behind her.
She came to me and placed her fingers on my eyelids
and they opened again to see the altar once more.
She was there, now beside it.
Standing before me, the Lady smiled
and the candlelight danced on her silver jewelry
and her dark eyes.
She stretched out a bangled hand to me.
Navy velvet spilled down around her arm like water
and I was caught in the wake,
being drawn to her the way ships are pulled out to sea.
Panic grabbed my feet then, and I found them on the floor
between the beats of my racing heart.
I ran from the room and slammed the door.
When I opened it again, she was gone.

Hekate's Devotion

by Shay Morgan

Blessed be the dark maiden
She who was born of the night
goddess trinity
reigning over the underworld, the celestial heavens and the deep earth
Hekate, lady who walks in darkness
hail unto thee
guide of the Elysian fields
keeper of the keys of all the universe
guardian of the crossroads of fate
she who bears the blade that cuts the silver cords of life and death
Goddess of ancient wisdom, mistress of magick
By the serpent who carries the wisdom of the chthonic earth, I pray
by the black she hound who howls beneath the holy moon, I pray
by the night mare who runs wild with lunatic prophetic vision, I pray
Evohe Hekate, mother of witches
My goddess, my queen, my beautiful darkness
In thy honour, I burn this sacred flame

Hekate's Deipna and Other Devotional Acts

by Venus Clark

Hekate's Deipna are meal offerings made to Hekate at the triple crossroads on the last night of each lunar month. In its most basic form today one can simply make offerings to her on this night, if that's all your circumstances will allow. However the event itself is much more elaborate and I encourage you to do as much as you can.

Preparation

First, you should clean Hekate's altar or the area where you will honor her (this would be your main altar if you use one for all the Gods). This can be done earlier in the day or right before the ritual. I find doing it earlier adds to the anticipation of the coming rite and lends an air of festivity. Save what you clear away because it will be part of her offering. Depending on the substance it can be burnt in a charcoal burner or added to the plate of food. Some examples of things you may gathering in your cleaning are dirt, dust, candle drippings, bits of cloth or string, etc. Another part of the pre-ritual clear out is pulling together anything left over from the previous month's offerings. For example if you made libations of wine but still have some left over in the bottle you should offer this to Hekate. Likewise if you had a bowl of barley and used only a portion the rest should be offered to Hekate. This process clears out the old month entirely. Everything will be burnt or go into the dinner.

For the ritual itself you will need an offering plate and incense burner, charcoal briquette, and incense at the very least. I also like to have a candle, wine, libation cup, and an image of Hekate – a statue or framed picture (even one printed from the internet will suffice). And of course, Hekate's supper. Traditionally the supper contains a sweet bread or cake, fish (sprat and mullet), garlic, eggs, and cheese. You can offer any or all of these as well as anything else you feel appropriate – for example, this is UPG but Hekate let me know she likes black olives so I usually include them. You should have everything ready beforehand to use during the ritual. Most charcoal briquettes will need several minutes to light and then a few more minutes before they are ready to use.

The Rite

You may start with a self-purification, such as dipping your hands in khernips. Approach the altar, light her candle if you're offering one, and spend a few moments in contemplation. When you are ready, speak some words of praise or a hymn such as the Orphic Hymn to Hekate or passage 409ff. from Hesiod's *Theogony*. I've adapted her hymn from PGM IV 2520-2569 for use in this ritual.

If you have anything from your cleaning to burn you should place it on the charcoal first. Then add some incense. Pour a libation if you're offering one. And finally present her supper. You may say something like, "Hekate, I offer to you this incense, this wine, this (name each item)... Look kindly upon these offerings and accept them with joyous heart."

You can end the rite here or continue with the theme of cleansing and purification at the end of the month.

Purification

Prayer for purification: "Hekate, look kindly upon your supplicant who brings you offerings on this day as on many days in the past. Mighty Hekate, please take the foul and filth from this place. Clear it of all negativity and harm." This can be followed by fumigating your home. Place incense or herbs on the charcoal and carry the burner around the home – be careful, it will be hot and you may need protection for your hands! Make a circuit that brings you back to the altar. There you may make a prayer for Hekate's protection during the new month, like: "Hekate Propylaia, please grant me (us/my family/etc., as appropriate) your protection and keep all harm from entering my (our) home. For this I am (we are) eternally grateful."

When you have completed the ritual, gather the supper up and dispose of it. This should be at a triple crossroad but do the best you can. In some circumstances people are only able to place it outside in their yard or even just indoors in its own trash bag that is taken out immediately.

Finally, this is a good time to perform divination, especially if you specifically desire to ask Hekate about something.

Other devotional acts

In addition to Hekate's Suppers, there are many things one can do to honor Hekate on a regular basis. First you may want to erect an altar in your home. This can take the form of the ancient *hekataia*, which should be placed either outside your front door or right inside it depending on your living situation. The shape it takes is up to you – place it on a shelf, a table, the floor, in a garden bed next to your front door, etc. This is an altar focusing on her role as protector and key bearer, so you may choose to decorate it along that theme. Be sure to 'feed' the *hekataia* with regular offerings, no less than once a month but preferably more frequently. You can speak a prayer to her as you enter or leave your home, passing by the *hekataia*, and may even leave a small offering at this time.

Hekate is a diverse Goddess with many attributes, as seen in her epithets and hymns. A good way to get to know her is to focus on one attribute at a time and to break the hymns down to small portions you focus on bit by bit. I suggest a minimum of one week for each but a month also makes a nice period and ties in well with her monthly dinners! You may also tie this in with the season or time of year – for example, winter is a very dark season in Britain and I like to focus on her light-bringing capabilities as the dark season drags on into February seeming without end. Some may prefer to focus on darker functions in the dark seasons and lighter in the light – there is no right or wrong. Find out what works for you.

If you'd like to do something special to honor Hekate or feel closer to her here are a few suggestions:

*Provide a loving home to a dog in need or volunteer at a shelter. Dogs are sacred to Hekate and are closely linked to her in many ways.

*You can care-take an abandoned or deserted place – whether urban or rural. A lonely stretch of river front or woods, an empty city lot, an abandoned house in your neighbourhood…Hekate frequents these places and because they are deserted doesn't mean they must be covered in trash.

*Take a walk at night and focus on Hekate as you do. You may try saying her name aloud, reciting a hymn, or praying to her while you walk. Modern street lights stand in for her torches, offering light and protection among the dark stretches of road. In my experience, if you take the time to notice, her presence is fully palpable along the road.

Helpful resources:

The Orphic Hymns. Athanassakis, A.
The Greek Magical Papyri in Translation. Betz, Hans Deiter (ed.)
Theogony. Hesiod
The Goddess Hekate. Ronan, Stephen (ed.)

To Hecate

by Hearthstone

Hecate I praise, fair maiden of the crossroad,
you who see things hidden, who heard Persephone
as she cried out from the underworld. Hecate,
with whose help did Demeter regain her dear child;
whose torches light the moonless night; who guards the gate;
who receives due offering wherever three roads meet;
yours, goddess, are shares in all the realms. Hecate,
who travels freely along all roads, I praise you.
To you, Hecate, are the mysteries known.
To you do women ever turn for protection.
To you do those who work magic pray for wisdom.
Hecate, ancient one, I praise and honor you.

A Prayer to Hekate

by Kenn Payne

Like the half waxed moon
You are both darkness and light;
What is known and what is kept hidden.
You show us the door, you give us the key
But only we can open it and pass through.
You wait at the threshold to light our path
Guiding, protecting, illuminating.
You shine a light on that which we refuse to accept
You make us see that which is not necessary,
To burn it away with your fiery brands
Bathing that space with the warm glow of your light –
Your love.
Fathomless Goddess; you who burn, scourge and cut away the bonds,
At whose grace we can know the secrets of ourselves.
Most misunderstood Lady who brings change;
You have lit my path,
Watched my back,
Guarded my door,
Soothed my pain,
Bestowed your gifts,
Listened to my prayers,
Shown me the way.
It is a long journey still ahead of me
But you are both within and without.
And I thank you.

To Hekate

by Emily Carding

Hekate, this name we gift you,
You who are older than names,
We visit you, in your deep places,
Your roots in the stars,
And ruddy feet
In the blood and bones of the primal surging Earth and waters,
The brilliance of a star veiled in darkness,
And once more robed in light,
You are the maiden Mother,
And know our needs and our not-needs,
Which are stripped away
In the craggy rebirth of rock and bloody tears.

You are the many layered apple-seed that dwells within,
And the warm light without,
containing too all the darkness,
It needs to grow into the tree of knowledge.
With your torch you guide us,
With your key you give us the power to choose,
To unlock,
Or simply bear the symbol
Of a path that is walked towards a gate unopened.
The third hand cuts away,
With sharpened knife,
All that holds us back.

We are left undone, unmade, unfinished,
With the knowledge of incompleteness,
We are given choice,
We are given voice,
And with the voice of choice,
We are given power.

Horse hooves lead us on a path of movement true and strong,
Serpentine stealth may teach us ways into hidden places,
And secret knowledge,
Dog-Wolf protector is ever loyal and full of instinct,

Not to be betrayed.
You give us choice,
And in the storm-filled darkness, you light the way,

Great Goddess, Dark Mother, shining Hekate!

Celebrating the Deipnon

Introduction

In Greek, deipnon means the evening meal, usually the largest meal of the day. Hekate's Deipnon is, at its most basic, a meal served to Hekate and the restless dead once a lunar month. This article sets forth: 1) a brief history including the practices of Hekate's Deipnon in antiquity; 2) a small (and necessarily incomplete) summation of Hekate as She relates to Her Deipnon; and 3) some of the more common ways Hellenic Polytheists celebrate the Deipnon today. This article makes no claim to be a complete, all-inclusive, or a formal scholarly work. When possible, sources are noted and historical facts are separated from opinion.

Hekate

The Titan Hekate, the "Worker From Afar," was born from the Titans Perses, the "Destroyer," and Asteria, "Starry One," who was a sister to Leto. This parentage grants Hekate dominion over oracular communion with the ghosts of the dead while Her cousin, Apollo, presides over oracles inspired by the heavens with prophetic powers granted by Zeus.

The Earth, Sea, and Sky

Hekate, in the time of the Golden Age of Titans, ruled in the heavens, on the Earth, and in the sea. Unlike all other Titans, Her authority did not diminish with the ascendency of the Olympians.

> "The son of Kronos did her no wrong nor took anything away of all that was her portion among the former Titan gods: but she holds, as the division was at the first from the beginning, privilege both in earth, and in heaven, and in sea. Also, because she is an only child, the goddess receives not less honor, but much more still, for Zeus honors her." – Hesiod, *Theogony* 404

This resulted in Her keeping the power to grant or withhold wealth, wise counsel, victory, good luck to sailors and hunters, prosperity, and increases in flocks and herds based on what She thought each individual deserved.

"For to this day, whenever any one of men on earth offers rich sacrifices and prays for favor according to custom, he calls upon Hekate. Great honor comes full easily to him whose prayers the goddess receives favorably, and she bestows wealth upon him; for the power surely is with her...Whom she will she greatly aids and advances: she sits by worshipful kings in judgment, and in the assembly whom she will is distinguished among the people. And when men arm themselves for the battle that destroys men, then the goddess is at hand to give victory and grant glory readily to whom she will. Good is she also when men contend at the games, for there too the goddess is with them and profits them: and he who by might and strength gets the victory wins the rich prize easily with joy, and brings glory to his parents. And she is good to stand by horsemen, whom she will: and to those whose business is in the gray uncomfortable sea, and who pray to Hekate and the loud-crashing Earth-Shaker, easily the glorious goddess gives great catch, and easily she takes it away as soon as seen, if so she will. She is good in the byre with Hermes to increase the stock. The droves of kine and wide herds of goats and flocks of fleecy sheep, if she will, she increases from a few, or makes many to be less." – Hesiod, *Theogony* 404

The Crossroads

So closely was Hekate associated with the crossroads that a common epithet for Her is Trioditis "of the Three Ways" or "of the Crossroads." The crossroads were viewed as places where spirits bent on vengeance were able to emerge, especially on the darkest night, the night of the new moon. On this night, with Hekate leading the revel-rout, accompanied by the howls of Stygian dogs, souls could cause great evil to befall whomever they came upon. As a result, She is described as a mighty and terrible divinity, ruling over the souls of the dead.[1]

As the door of many homes opened to a crossroads (the path from the home which intersected with the street), most homes had a shrine to Hekate built into the wall adjacent to their gate or doorway. Offerings and prayers were placed there to protect the family from evil influences and to ask for Hekate's blessings on the household.[2] The members of the household also sought oracle reading from the shrines. While it is not clear how this was accomplished as the small shrine was unattended, it could be that omens were read there.[3]

Hekate is the Kore's guide to and from Her Husband's House and, as such, She played an important role in the Mysteries at Eleusis. This is a crossroads of life into death and death into life. While knowledge concerning the Mysteries at Eleusis is limited, we do know that those who were initiated no longer feared death and were the happiest of people.

> "Beautiful indeed is the Mystery given us by the blessed gods: death is for mortals no longer an evil, but a blessing." – inscription found at Eleusis

This lack of specific knowledge concerning the Mysteries of Eleusis opens the door to individual theories. Hekate's role in the Mysteries, in my opinion, is signaled by the two torches She carries. Statues of Hekate lighting the way line the walls of the temple at Eleusis. Imagine you have died and find yourself at the cross point of a three-way path. Your life is the path behind you. Hekate is directly in front of you where the path makes a V. Her torches, since you have learned the Mysteries, reveal both paths. One path leads to evil, the other leads to happiness and blessings. If you have not been through the Mysteries, you may be fated to stay at the crossroads, becoming one of the restless spirits that emerge from the crossroads to wreak havoc in the mortal world, or you may stumble onto the path that leads to evil, or you may be lucky and find the blessed path.

I believe this offers a viable explanation for the thread that connects Hekate to the revel-routs of restless souls at the crossroads and the Mysteries of Eleusis.

Purification and Expiation

Less commonly known about the Titan is that She, like her cousin Apollon, could offer purification and expiation for those who committed bad deeds. Generally, but not exclusively, expiation at the Deipnon was for minor bad deeds within the household. One such ritual performed at the Deipnon required all the household members to touch a dog, which was then sacrificed to Hekate as a scapegoat.

Murder attracted Her special attention. She, and the vengeful spirit of the person murdered, would inflict madness on the criminal until he or she atoned for the crime.

History and Practices of the Deipnon

The main purpose of the Deipnon was to honor Hekate and to placate the souls in her wake who "longed for vengeance."[4] A secondary purpose was to purify the household and to atone for bad deeds a household member may have committed that offended Hekate, causing Her to withhold Her favor from them.

This was done the night before the first visible sliver of moon could be seen, the night of the new moon.[5] The new moon was the last day of the lunar month and the Deipnon rituals allowed the family to begin the new month, which they celebrated as the Noumenia, purified.[6] This differs from how modern astronomy calculates the new moon, so one may not follow a modern calendar to set this date.

The Deipnon consists of three main parts: 1) the meal that was set out at a crossroads, 2) an expiation sacrifice, and 3) purification of the household.

The Meal

The specific foods mentioned most often in primary sources are those usually associated with offerings for the dead: raw eggs, some type of small cake, garlic, leeks and/or onions, and fish.[7] The meal was set out at a crossroads after sunset. Most families placed the meal on top of or inside the small shrine to Hekate they had outside of their door.

After the meal was set out, the person placing it did not look back at it, believing the restless spirits who dined became angry at anyone who looked at them; those who looked back could be driven insane.

Although it was considered sacrilegious, and would invite Hekate's wrath, it was a common practice for persons in extreme poverty to do eat the meal.[8]

> "Ask Hekate whether it is better to be rich or starving; she will tell you that the rich send her a meal every month [food placed inside her door-front shrines] and that the poor make it disappear before it is even served." – Aristophanes, *Plutus* 410 (trans. O'Neill)

Expiation

As previously discussed, in order to atone for acts committed by the household, some of which they might not even be aware of, a dog was sacrificed to Hekate as a scapegoat.[9] According to the Merriam-Webster Dictionary a scapegoat is "one that bears the blame for others." Prior to the sacrifice taking place, each member of the household touched the dog, transmitting all of their bad deeds onto this sacred animal of Hekate. Once the dog was sacrificed, the head of the family read the entrails to be sure the sacrifice was accepted and any act of offense against the Titan or the Gods was wiped clean. This ritual allowed the family to go forward into the new month free of pollution.

Purification

Purification of the household had two parts: 1) fumigation; and 2) the removal of "leftovers" from offerings and sacrifices. Fumigation was accomplished by carrying a baked clay censer of incense throughout the house and property. The clay censer was then deposited at the crossroads or shrine as an offering and was never used again.[10] It was considered a "leftover" from the ritual. Other such leftovers included; incense ashes and the ashes from sacrifices that were on the family altar, waste blood,[11] and any remaining food that had fallen onto the floor. Food that falls to the floor was never to be picked up as it had passed to Hekate, who would redistribute it to the spirits.[12]

> "Whatever is thrown or dropped is lost to this world, whatever is caught is gained" – Pausanias, *Description of Greece I*, 17, 3; Aelius Spartianus, Hadrian XXVI, 7.

This suggests how the poor may have been able to eat the meals without incurring Hekate's wrath. If the poor were able to snatch the meal up before it was set down, before it was "lost" to the spirits and to Hekate, it would be their "gain."

All of the leftovers were deposited at the shrine or a crossroads, preferably at the same time as the meal since you were not to look back at it. Then the household shut its doors and retired for the night. As it was considered unlucky to pick up, touch, or step on these offerings,[13] I am uncertain on how the offerings were dealt with the following days. The offerings may have been left in place or the prohibition on touching them may have expired following a set length of time.

Current Practices

Current methods of observing the Deipnon mix traditional forms of ritual with new. In some cases, the new ritual practices are due to adapting to modern life in a very different culture than that of ancient Athens. Other practices arise out of differing interpretations of Hekate's significance. Some knowledge has been lost and some history is no longer intuitively understood. From what others share about how they celebrate the Deipnon, there is less of a focus on placation and warding the home from evil spirits and an increased focus on making an offering to Hekate and performing acts of charity. Sacrificing a dog is currently illegal in the USA. Scapegoating, to my knowledge, is no longer performed even in a "bloodless" way. The element of expiation has been completely omitted from the Deipnon. Below is a sampling of what modern coreligionists do to observe the Deipnon.

The Meal

This offering is one of the more common ritual elements in current practice. Eggs, onions, garlic, and leeks are still placed on plates and offered. It's not unheard of for incense to take the place of food as the meal offering.

While the make-up of the meal has remained intact, the location of the offering often differs from traditional placement. Almost no one has a shrine to Hekate where their sidewalk or driveway meets the street in front of their home. While many still seek out a crossroads, others place the meal on a central altar in their home or apartment for a day and then dispose of the offering later. Others place the offering on a plate that rests on a rock in a pool of water, neatly bringing together the three areas over which Hekate rules.

There is much less worry about looking back at the plate once it has been placed or about vengeful spirits driving one mad if not placated. Modern discussions center on what constitutes "proper disposal" of the offering the next day. Burial of the offering is preferred whenever possible, but some place it in the trash or in a composter. Persons who place the meal outside say they have not needed to dispose of the offering as it is usually gone by morning.

Cleaning or Sweeping the House

While offering the sweepings from the home is still done, what is in the sweepings can be much different from ancient Athens. No longer do we allow dropped food to stay on the floor for weeks. People currently do not have ashes from sacrificed animals, dog carcasses, or waste blood in homes and apartments. Stubs from candles used in rituals, ashes from incense, and other previous offerings can find their way into the pile of "sweepings," which is offered on the Deipnon, as this is a time when some Hellenic Polytheists clean off all home altars and shrines. Cleaning out a refrigerator or pantry is becoming a common practice.

Charity

Although the purpose of the meal offered at the Deipnon was not intended to feed the poor in antiquity, current offerings of food or money to local food banks in Hekate's name are an expression of charity designed to do precisely that – feed the hungry. Donating time at a soup kitchen serving meals is another act of charity and goodwill done to observe the Deipnon. Not only do Hellenic Polytheists believe this is an ethical act keeping with Hellenic virtues, they are giving in Hekate's name so She may find them worthy of Her blessings of prosperity, wisdom, and increase. This is not viewed as a quid pro quo, but a reciprocation of favors that build a stronger bond.

Other practices are resolving personal and/or financial obligations and emptying and cleaning a special jar kept in a pantry or on an altar in honor of Zeus Ktesios. Both practices are based on the same general concept – to close out the old month and enter the new month fresh. That fresh start is celebrated the next day during the Noumenia when it is auspicious to start new projects and unspoiled contents are placed back into the Ktesios jar.

Summary

Information on the historical observance of the Deipnon is spotty at best and spread throughout many primary sources, making it difficult for modern coreligionists to obtain accurate information on this important and basic household ritual. As increasingly concise information is more widely disseminated and more Hellenic Polytheists incorporate this ritual into their spiritual lives, it will be interesting to see an evolution of the continued rituals and also to see if those participating find the Deipnon to be as fulfilling and important as their religious and cultural ancestors did.

---

[1] Apollon. Rhod. iii. 529, 861, iv. 829; Theocrit. *l. c.* ; Ov. *Heroid.* xii. 168, *Met.* xiv. 405; Stat. *Theb.* iv. 428 ; Virg. *Aen.* iv. 609; Orph. *Lith.* 45, 47; Eustath. *ad Hom.* p. 1197, 1887; Diod. iv. 45.

[2] Aristoph. *Vesp.* 816, *Lysistr.* 64; Eurip. *Med.* 396; Porphyr. *de Abstin.* ii. 16; Hesych. *s. v.* Hekataia

[3] Aristoph. *Vesp.* 816, *Lysistr.* 64; Eurip. *Med.* 396; Porphyr. *de Abstin.* ii. 16; Hesych. *s. v.* Hekataia

[4] Plutarch (Moralia, 709 A)

[5] Aristophanes (Plutus, 594)

[6] Rodhe, i 234 n., and references.

[7] Antiphanes, in Athenaeus, 313 B (2. 39 K), and 358 F; Melanthius, in Athenaeus, 325 B. Plato, Com. (i. 647. 19 K), Apollodorus, Melanthius, Hegesander, Chariclides (iii. 394 K), Antiphanes, in Athenaeus, 358 F; Aristophanes, Plutus, 596.

[8] Cinesias, in Plutarch, Moralia, 170 B.

[9] Hekate's Suppers, by K. F. Smith.

[10] Roscher, 1889; Heckenbach, 2781; Rohde, ii. 79, n. 1.

[11] Ammonius (p. 79, Valckenaer)

[12] Diels, *Fragmente der Vorsokratiker*, 1:463; Diogenes Laertius, *Lives of Eminent Philosophers* VIII, 34.

[13] Petronius, 134

Charge of the Dark Queen

I am your master who rides the night sky.
three-faced mother of abominable mothers
light hunter, dragon Graal, the first witch,
ever-shifting all and none!

My power has no limits and infinite penalty.
Call me Diana, Lunata or all-gifted Hecate
it matters not.

You cannot help but see me, love me and fear me.
For I am the liege of all worlds
divine whore and berated virgin
bubbling and frothing in darkest dreams!
I will never be dominated,
for I am no spinster!

Nay!

Toy with me at the cost of your soul.
Be disemboweled or refined as I see fit!
Or embrace me...
And know wonders as you have never known!
Drink deep of my distilled abyss,
suckle upon my acrimonious blood-waters of salt and wine
cry as you are reborn!

The stars themselves obey my commands
for I am the devourer and maker of galaxies
they are my cloak of fate
circling about you,
as I weave my beautiful and terrible spells
on Terra,
this world of men.

Rise,
look your mother-lover in the eye if you dare!
Gaze upon my fell beauty,
hold my hand and soar through the cosmos;

for my gift is the magick
that which will challenge you
as nothing else ever has done!

I was with you,
drenched in aching ecstasy,
as the first man and woman made love.
I wept with you,
donning scarlet armor and sword
seething in anger at the purple and red wounds
as the first man forced himself on his mate.

as you battle the detestation of this dying world
know that my magick will nourish you and guard you all
once you were weak and oppressed,
now becoming the empowered and gifted.
as darkness menstruates upon the moon,
my face is revealed
and my heartbeat is yours.

Aoros

by Rebecca Buchanan

It was his knife that caught her eye. It looked like the one that had killed her.

Cleopatra's Fountain was one of Phoebe's favorite places in the city. Tucked away behind a small market, around a curve and then around another curve away from any major streets, it was always quiet. Lovers occasionally met here, but most people seem to have forgotten about it. The Pharaoh would have been disappointed. Had she been the ninth Cleopatra or the tenth? They all blended together after a while. She had been so proud of the park when it was first built; her gift to the city for remaining loyal in the face of open revolt. Lemon and lime and persimmon trees, graceful marble benches, and the fountain in the center, now lichen-stained, a playful nymph pouring water from a pitcher.

Phoebe liked to sit on the edge of the fountain and watch the moon rise in the water. And only the moon. The absence of her reflection had bothered her the first few decades – though she was rather glad that she could not see the cut across her throat. This night, the moon was a thin waning sliver. Tomorrow it would be dark. The rapist would have struck again, then. Thank the Gods the City Guard had finally realized the significance of those henbane and poppy seeds she had the wind drop, and tracked the rapist to the herb market. He would be dead and his soul in Tartaros by midday –

– unless his family could raise a large enough bribe. Then the Governor would commute his sentence from death to exile and he would become another city's problem...and another aoros's problem.

A small scratch of sound.

Phoebe looked up to see a cloaked figure standing at the edge of the park, partially hidden by an overgrown lemon tree. Definitely male, and quite tall. Phoebe tilted her head. Probably here to meet his lover. She returned to watching the sliver of moon, and let her fingers draw circles in the water.

Another sound, a bit louder. This time two figures emerged from the twisting streets; one moved with purpose, the other with a touch of uncertainty. They moved up beside the first figure, pushing branches aside. Hushed whispers slid across the stone and grass...a name...? The whispers began to jump and skip, agitated.

She stood and took a step closer, then two – then stopped, paralyzed with memory at the wink of silver and amber beneath the cloak of the tall man. A knife. She knew that knife. A hand rose to touch the cut and thin trickles of blood across her throat....

*****

The city had been young then, its temples shining new in the sun. The slavers had come in secret, disguised as pilgrims come to pray and make offers at the Heraeum. No one had realized who they were until that evening, when children and young women failed to return home. Fourteen total, some as young as five, snatched from the market or the temple courtyards or their own front door steps – including her own sister, Cori. Only one little boy had been reclaimed, found by an uncle in a port city leagues distant.

We need a protector, the City Council had decided. Someone who can defend us from these threats which we cannot see. So they had prayed and chanted and made offerings to Hera and they were given their answer in omens of peacocks and plump cows. But they had not wanted to believe that answer, so they prayed to Zeus – and the Thunderer told them the same, in omens of lightning and hail. Still, they refused to believe something so terrible, so they traveled to Delphi, where Apollon's priestess, in a sing-song voice, told them that another sister must be lost for the city's remaining daughters and sons to be safe.

She had broken her father's heart when she volunteered; his hair turned gray. Her mother took to her bed and refused to eat. Her brother cried. For Cori, she tried to explain. But they could not say good-bye to another daughter. Even on the day of her sacrifice.

She remembered the knife, and the priest of Hekate. He had been so old, his joints swollen, that his apprentice had to slit her throat while the older man prayed and whispered and chanted and called on the Dread Goddess, The Watcher, The Walker of Borders, to bless the city with a guardian.

And then nothing. Nothing at all. Until she opened her eyes to bright stars and a dark moon. She was alone on the acropolis, the doors to the temples all closed, the priests and priestesses asleep on their mats, the crowd gone.

She went home, but her gray-haired father and mother could not see her, nor her little brother. The cat mewed and hissed at her, though, constantly, until her mother finally threw it outside. Being with them grew too painful, so she took to wandering the streets. And one dusk, she came upon the old priest of Hekate, who looked straight at her and said "The crossroads. The crossroads."

The Goddess came to the crossroads that midnight, with Her terrible hounds, and from Her Phoebe learned what it meant to be an aoros; to weave wind and water with her hands; to make the earth dance with her steps; to speak with the creatures of the night who so often saw and heard what men did not.

And she trapped a burglar with snarling dogs until the City Guard could haul him away. And exposed the healer who sold false medicines. And set the cats on the rats who would have brought plague.

Her family died, eventually, one by one. First her father, than her mother, then her brother and his children. Each time, she caught a glimpse of the beloved departing soul, wrapped in Hermes' warm black wings. Until everyone who knew her name was gone. But she remained, aoros, sworn guardian and protector.

*****

Phoebe shook her head, dropped her hand from the bubbles of blood. Nearly thirteen centuries. That knife was long lost, thrown away or buried. It could not be the same knife. Just a bit alike. Not the same knife.

She took a step closer. The tall man bent, pushed a branch heavy with lemons out of the way, and she recognized him. Iason, son of Leiandros. He often accompanied his uncle, Zenobios, to sessions of the City Council. Zenobios was known to be a wise and pragmatic man, and it was widely expected that Iason would take his place when he had grown too old to serve.

" –oolish, Aristides."

The shorter man stuttered. "I am merely expressing a legitimate concern, Iason. If the Pharaoh learns of our involvement – "

"He will not." The third man this time. Rounder than the other two, and dressed in fur and silk; too heavy for a warm night such as this. "The Pharaoh's only concerns are peace and taxes. So long as those are plentiful – and timely – he doesn't care who is Governor."

"Agreed." Iason gave a sharp nod. Phoebe stepped closer to him, looking up into his hood as he continued. Amber eyes. "My uncle is the logical choice to succeed Prokopios. Denys, is your man in position – and can he be trusted?"

"Yes. It took my last coin, but he has been well-compensated. And he will be out of the city before the Governor stops breathing. I assume that my debts will be forgiven by the new Governor, and that I, too, will be justly compensated...."

Iason half-bowed. "Of course." He held out a thin blue philter, which Denys quickly palmed. "My uncle heeds my counsel, and I will speak to him on your behalf."

"Couldn't we just...." Aristides breathed in hard. "Couldn't we just humiliate Prokopios? Publicly? Have him sent into exile?"

"He could always come back. Do you really want Prokopios in the Governor's seat? The man thinks you're an idiot. Remember when he

124

publicly humiliated *you*? Called your design for the new Heraeum as graceless and ugly as a drunkard's pigsty?"

Aristides went red.

"So now it is Tychon's name which will be praised to the ages. And what do you think the chances are that he will award you the new gymnasium – "

"Yes! Very well! Tomorrow, at the banquet." Aristides turned, breaking lemon branches, crack crack crack, as he stomped away.

Denys grinned and bowed to Iason. "Tomorrow. And do not forget your promise."

Iason bowed, too. "Of course."

Denys turned and disappeared down a winding alley. Iason took a few steps down a different path, then stopped. As Phoebe watched, he returned to the park, paused for a moment in front of the lichen-covered fountain, and then tossed in a bronze coin.

Phoebe waited until he was gone and then went over to the fountain herself. The nymph smiled at her. The coin glittered dully at the bottom of the water. The moon had moved. She looked up, arching her neck. It was nearly at its zenith. She would be at the crossroads at midnight, as She was at every crossroads at every midnight.

Phoebe turned and ran from the park, dodging between lime and persimmon trees. Around a curve in the road, then another curve, past the market, down the hill and down some more, around the old gymnasium, then straight down the hill to the crossroads. The city's original border marker stood at its center, a triangular pillar taller than two men. The face of a woman was carved into each side; they had grown indistinct with time, but Phoebe remembered them as they had looked new.

The sounds of frogs and bugs, and a distant owl. Bats high above.

The city had been much smaller then. It had covered only the acropolis, a bit of the slope, and the field below, where grains and fruits were cultivated. The marker had been placed here, at the edge of those fields.

She looked over her shoulder. The city was much larger now. It covered the entire hill and spread across the fields far to the south and east. Not so much to the west; no one wanted to build near the marker. Offerings were still left, though; her nose wrinkled at the sweet stink of decaying honey cakes and souring milk.

A distant, fierce howl. Then a second, and a third, four, five, six, seven, eight, nine...

The cerberi were upon her, three triple-headed hounds, nearly the size of horses. Each head with black or red or white eyes and tongues to match. Yipping, snarling, whining, they raced around her. One cerberus ran off into the field, sending sleeping birds to agitated flight.

Another nosed around the pillar, snapping up the cakes and milk. The third ran right up to her, sniffing.

How they had terrified her at first. Now, she reached out a hand and gently touched one great head on the nose; white eyes blinked at her. The other two heads whimpered and butted against her chest and thigh, demanding ear scratches.

Phoebe laughed, obliging. "And how are you this evening?" The cerberus whimpered from three great throats, tail thumping. His whole body shook with excitement. She laughed again.

Her laugh was cut off by a high, angry wail. Not the hounds this time. Nine great heads rose up, ears perked, looking back towards the east. And they were off, one cerberus bounding out of the fields as the three dogs took off towards the west, yowling, announcing the Goddess' approach.

Phoebe could see the torches, glowing with promethean fire. She fell to her knees, head down, eyes closed. Even dead, it was painful to look upon a Goddess.

The light grew stronger, and the wails grew louder. Angry, desperate cries by souls who had died after living pointless, unfulfilled lives; a river of pain and denial, and hunger for a life never lived.

The torchlight burned through her closed eyelids. Soft laughter.

"Phoebe, you are aoros, one of my favored. Stand."

Phoebe rose, wincing as she opened her eyes. The Goddess could change Her form at will, but She was always beautiful, and that beauty always burned. Tonight, She was barefoot, a simple white gown covering Her from shoulders to ankles – not unlike the sacrificial gown that she herself wore, Phoebe noticed. Her face was that of a maiden and Her eyes – Phoebe blinked, looked away, looked up again – were the black of primal darkness, of the deepest trough of the ocean; so easy to fall into that darkness. And Her hair was alive, each strand a tiny iridescent serpent, green gold purple blue, tongues darting. They shifted and slithered, some peering at Phoebe, some basking in the warmth of the torches, some hissing the ghosts into silence.

The Goddess stepped closer, the torches which floated to either side of Her following, bobbing gently. Phoebe saw the puppy then, cradled in Her hands. One over-sized ear fell over an eye. It was an ordinary puppy, not a cerberus; a sacrifice left at some crossroads altar. "It has been some time since you sought Me out. You have grown accustomed to your existence as aoros. But I remember, for many months after your death, when you could not go a night without seeking My comfort and counsel."

"Yes, Torchbearer, for which I am humbly grateful. And I seek Your counsel again this night."

The Goddess was silent. The puppy whimpered and nuzzled closer.

"There is a plot. To murder Governor Prokopios and replace him with Zenobios."

The Goddess nodded, once. "Yes."

"I am uncertain....Prokopios is a venal, greedy man. He has betrayed his oaths to protect this city's people more than once. But he does not imprison the people unjustly or take unwilling women to his bed, as some Governors do. Zenobios, from what I have seen, is honorable; he makes sure the City Guard is well-funded and the wells remain clean. But, I am reluctant to allow even an honorable man to take power in such a terrible way – especially if Iason will be whispering in his ear. And what if Iason does not intend for his uncle to remain in power? What if the Pharaoh in Alexandria discovers the plot? What will he do to the city? Will he see it as a sign of rebellion and send an army?" She twisted her fingers. "Gatekeeper, I don't know what to do."

The Goddess laughed, and the puppy whined. "And you came to Me for the answer? To be told what to do? To solve your problem for you?" The Dread Goddess shook Her head. She set down the puppy, which proceeded to trip over its own ears in its eagerness to chase after a bug. "You are the aoros. You are the guardian spirit of this place, this city and its people. You chose this, willingly. Thirteen centuries ago, you stood atop that hill and swore an oath to all the Gods, by all the Gods, by Gaea Herself, to remain so long as stone stood atop stone, so long as one man or woman or child called this place home, and to protect them. And then your blood was spilled beneath My altar and you were bound as aoros. Willingly." The Goddess crouched and gently picked up the puppy. "I will not tell you what to do, child. You must make a decision – and accept the consequences."

The Goddess strode forward, towards the west. The torches flared, smokeless divine fire warm and bright. Phoebe stepped back, off the road, into the field. The ghosts followed, wailing and crying and sneering, echoes of people old and young; they trailed along behind the Goddess, pleading to return to the lives they had never really lived. The Goddess ignored them. Phoebe could only watch them, with pity and disgust.

As the river of souls flowed away towards the horizon, she heard the Lightbringer in her ear. "You are favored, child. I would not have accepted your offering of yourself if you lacked the will and intelligence to serve Me, and your people."

Silence, then, accept for frogs and humming bugs. Phoebe looked up, searching for the moon. The thin sliver now hung in the western quarter of the sky. The morning star already glowed at the edge of the eastern horizon. It would be dawn soon.

In the dark of early morning, she set out, back up the hill, towards her city.

*****

Prokopios made his home in a brightly painted teal and orange mansion to the north of the acropolis. Its balconies offered a magnificent view of the temples (the Heraeum, the twin shrines to Apollon and Artemis, the temple to Zeus-Ammon with its massive gilded statue, the partial Iseum which would be the largest in the province upon completion). Those balconies were filled now with chattering and cackling and drunken guffaws. Artists and sculptors and poets and playwrights and priests and priestesses and the odd philosopher, sharing drinks and praise with the dozen or so men of the City Council and their wives and mistresses and the Governor himself. The Governor was accompanied by one pair of beautiful courtesans and another pair of thick-shouldered bull mastiffs.

Phoebe wandered the crowd, trailing in Denys' silken wake; he was a dozen different shades of brilliant blue. Servants, eyes downcast, held out platters and goblets of delicacies and sweets. He sampled each as he passed, burping in appreciation: baked spinach and feta cheese puffs, roast lamb with garlic and oregano, butter cookies, prawns, pistachios, and wines and beers made from a hundred different varieties of grape and peach and raspberry. She tried to remember what honey wine tasted like, and failed.

Iason and his uncle were in attendance, too, on the far side of the balcony from the Governor. Iason bent and whispered something to Zenobios; the older man frowned, then nodded.

A quick look around. No Aristides.

She turned her attention back to Denys. Did he have the poison on him? Or would the man he had hired bring it with him? Would it be in the Governor's wine or his soup or his food or his sweets? And where was this man that Denys spoke of? Was it a (humble) servant?

Phoebe scowled impatiently. The mastiffs growled, heads dropping. She hastily put a finger to her lips and shushed them. Prokopios dropped his hand to one head; the dogs whimpered and settled back down.

The courtesans, dark blonde and strawberry blonde, were laughing at something witty someone had said as Denys approached the Governor. "My lord, a splendid banquet, just splendid. I am honored at your invitation."

"Huh." Prokopios grinned, a mischievous spark lighting his eyes. "Denys, tell us one of your famous stories, and perhaps I shall knock a few drachmas off your debt. Tell us that one in which you swindled the

128

Governor of Athens out of his favorite racing horse." Prokopios laughed, and so did everyone else.

Denys' face was tight, but he forced a smile. Phoebe walked around him, circling the small party as he stuttered an answer. "I did not... *swindle*...the Governor, my lord. It was a trade, and I was smart enough to get out ahead. That is all. I don't swindle. No."

"Huh."

"Oh, my lord," the darker blonde courtesan pouted, "you're embarrassing him. See how his face turns red. Why, now it clashes horribly with his silken cloak."

"Hm, you're right, dearheart." The strawberry blonde on Prokopios' left nodded. "It would look so much better with your coloring."

More pouting, wheedling. "Do you think so?"

Prokopios grinned. "Not going to disappoint the ladies, are you, Denys?"

The latter's mouth twisted. Out of the corner of her eye, Phoebe watched as Iason and Zenobios moved around the room, greeting a few other members of the Council. With a rough twist of the clasp, Denys pulled off the cloak. A polite bow, and he handed it to the darker blonde courtesan. With a delighted laugh, she swirled it about her shoulders and turned in furious circles, the cloak flaring like bright blue wings. Prokopios applauded, and the crowd around him joined in.

"Here now, dearheart, you're all askew." The strawberry blonde courtesan patted and tugged her companion's clothing and hair back into place, straightened the emerald and gold necklace and earrings. "Peacock colors. You are like unto Hera, now."

One of the mastiffs barked, low and rumbly. Phoebe looked down at him. A second bark, a thump of his tail.

– a slim blue philter disappeared into the strawberry blonde's voluminous skirts.

"Well now," Phoebe breathed, "not a man." And in response to her breath the wind rose, pushing across the balcony. The startled poets and playwrights and mistresses bent their heads. "Hush." Phoebe slowly dropped her hands to her sides, and the wind settled.

She took a few steps, two, three, and knelt between the thick-legged mastiffs. She scratched their ears and they whined happily. "Soon." She watched, eyes never leaving the courtesan's hands. They fluttered and danced around the Governor's head, his shoulders, fed him bits of guinea fowl and lamb and sweet cake. And when one hand disappeared into the folds of her dress, Phoebe tensed, and the hand emerged, the fingers curled tight to hide –

"Now!"

129

The mastiffs leapt, teeth bared, fur standing straight. The courtesan screamed as they slammed into her side and back, crushing her to the marble floor. The crowd screamed, leaping away, tripping over one another. The blonde courtesan screamed and fainted, half draped across a chair. The Governor screamed, yelled at the mastiffs to heel, desist, stop!

The philter slid across the floor, disappearing among trampling feet.

Prokopios grabbed one mastiff by the scruff of his heavy neck, yanked and pulled. Guards were piling into the room, pushing philosophers out of their way. Phoebe raised her hands and the wind followed her gesture, blowing hard across the balcony, knocking over potted plants and sending lamps swinging wildly.

The poison. Where was – ah.

Phoebe dropped her hands, slowly, and the wind gradually dropped to a gentle breeze. Heads came back up, hair and clothes in disarray.

"What is this?" Zenobios reached down a spotted hand. Fingers thick with age closed painfully around the philter. He straightened, grunting, and held open his hand. Iason peered over his uncle's shoulder, expression one of curiosity. "She dropped it. When the dogs hit her."

Prokopios gave up trying to pull the mastiff off his mistress and leaned forward, nose wrinkled. His eyes darkened. "Well, dearheart...." He looked down at the strawberry blonde courtesan.

"Perfume," she gasped.

"Really." Disbelief stained his voice. He snatched the philter from Zenobios' palm and bent down towards her. "Care to wear some for me, then? I'm sure it has a lovely scent."

The courtesan was shaking her head, trying to back away, but held in place by the great mastiff. The second dog growled ominously and she stilled.

Phoebe cast her eyes around, searching for Denys. The guests were moving in, crowding that corner of the balcony, pressing shoulders and cheeks together, straining to see and hear. Impatiently, she sliced her hand and the wind cut through the mob; random bits of loose clothing flew off into the sky, and a few of the lamps. Even the guards cried out this time, raising their shields.

"Ah-ha." A rumpled bright blue splotch cowering behind a gilded bench. She pointed. "Him!" she commanded. The second mastiff leapt over his companion and the prone courtesan, lips pulled back in a snarl. Denys, one eye peering over his arm, cried out and scuttled backwards, and ran right into the bench. Thick legs spread wide, the dog shoved his head forward, growling, pinning the frightened man with his eyes.

130

Phoebe grinned. "Good boy." With a soft breath and a gentle wave, she stilled the wind.

Prokopios straightened slowly, eyes moving back and forth between the two dogs and their prisoners. "Huh," he said. He waggled his fingers. "Take her away. And him."

Guards, spears and swords and shields in hand, swarmed forward, pushing the mob out of the way. They hauled the courtesan to her feet, and she yelled and pleaded with Prokopios as they dragged her through the door. The Governor ignored her, watching as Denys was yanked upright. The guards began to shove him towards the same door, hitting him with the butts of their swords.

"I was not alone in this, Prokopios!" Denys screamed. He waved his hands, cringing as the guards beat them back down with their shields. "Iason! Iason, too! Aristides!" They were dragging him through the door behind the courtesan. "Iason planned to — "

The doors slammed shut. The crowd was still.

"Why that's absurd," Zenobios nearly spat. His voice shook with age and indignation. He placed his hand on Iason's shoulder and turned to Prokopios. "Governor, my nephew had nothing to do with this plot. Nothing whatsoever."

"Yes, he did," Phoebe snapped. The dogs, gathered once more at their master's legs, rumbled.

"I give you my word, my lord. He would have nothing to gain by your death. Iason is an honorable man. Denys, on the other hand... well, it is well-known that he is deeply in debt to you. Your death would have been of great relief to him. As for Aristides, well...." The old man shrugged.

Prokopios was silent, eyes jumping from the older man and the younger and back. He scratched one dog's head. "Huh," he finally said. He waved a guard over. "Execute the merchant and the whore at dawn." He leaned in closer and muttered into the guard's ear. "I believe that Denys still had several fine statues from his collection left. Bring them over at once." The guard nodded, bowed and departed.

"Damn," Phoebe muttered, foot pressing down hard onto the balcony. Beneath the mansion, the ground shook slightly.

*****

Their heads were hung on a spear at the crossroads, a warning to anyone else who might be plotting and a thanks to the Watcher for safekeeping the Governor (and his city and its people).

Phoebe glared up at the heads. She went over her plan in her mind again and again, gnawing at it, trying to remember every little detail of the previous night; trying to figure out where she had gone wrong.

Two conspirators dead, one safe, the fourth gone in the night, fleeing to Gods knew where.

She didn't hear the little girl. She smelled the honey cake. Phoebe looked down and there She was at her side, munching, lips honey-slick. Thick black hair loose in the wind. A puppy with ears too big for his head stumbled around Her feet, bumping into Her legs.

"Consider this a lesson," the Dread Goddess said, voice small and sweet. "A partial victory is still a partial failure. And if the future which Apollon has foreseen comes to pass...well, you cannot fail at all."

The Gatekeeper turned away and skipped down the road, puppy dancing at Her heels.

Contradiction in Terms

by Allyson Szabo

Young, old,
Shy, bold.
Hardly known,
Yet known by many.
She is the Lady of Contradictions.
Hecate Triformus,
With faces young and triple.
Hecate the Hag,
Of later years, and magic.
Hecate the Companion,
Friend to Persephone and Demeter.
Hecate the Keyholder,
Who allows the dead to move beyond.
Hecate Gatekeeper,
The one who presides over the Mysteries.
She herself is a mystery!

Hecate

by Vicki Scotti

Hecate light my way with your torches so bright
Hecate show the way through these crossroads with light
With your key open me, to the mysteries ahead
Hecate light my way at these crossroads I dread
Hecate light my way with your torches so bright
Hecate show the way through these crossroads with light
Bind me with cord so taut, birthing me as I grow
Hecate light my way at these crossroads I sow
Hecate light my way with your torches so bright
Hecate show the way through these crossroads with light
Hecate light my way at these crossroads I made

Daily Prayer for Guidance

by Krysta S. Roy

Blessed Goddess Hekate:
Please continue to show me the path I'm meant to walk,
And alert me to the choices open to me along the way,
So that I may fulfill my own chosen destiny,
And make the most of the talents and skills I've been given.

Please continue to guide me,
Through symbols and dreams,
Intuition and synchronicity,
And keep me safe and strong,
Healthy and inspired,
So that I may follow you, serve you,
And learn whatever you would teach me.

Please keep me under your watchful eye,
And your divine protection,
Lighting my way with your torches,
Surrounding me with a shield of light,
That I may walk with confidence,
Knowing that you guide me and guard me,
Now and always.

Seasons of the Witch: Hecate and the Wheel of the Year

by Leni Hester

Over the past decade and a half, I've been fortunate to have Hecate reveal herself to me during certain times of the year. Working with Hecate in a Wiccan context (as opposed to a Hellenic Reconstructionist context) has been very instructive and at times, challenging. Unlike many deities familiar to Wiccan practitioners, traditionally Hecate has no male consort. When evoking her into Wiccan circle, I have usually not called a God-form to accompany her; if I do, I call the god Saturn who has no link to her mythologically or historically, but who shares a similar energetic signature (choices, limitations, potentials, and change). They complement each other well, but it usually feels better and less forced to call Hecate alone.

I discovered early on that my awareness of Hecate's presence is dependent on the season, the moon phase and even the weather. I usually become aware of her presence in the weeks before Samhain. Sometime in mid-October, especially if it's a waning or new moon, I become aware of Hecate awakening. There's a strange feral excitement going into Samhain, the weather turning cool and the trees in brilliant color, the deepening shadows and lengthening dark. The whole world is retreating into sleep, but part of me is waking up, hungry and audacious. When I visualize her, she's running through gnarly woods with her wolves, or she's an elegant queen holding court in moonlit graveyards. Everything about her feels wild and mysterious. When I feel like that, I know Hecate is near and magick is afoot.

My Samhain observance always honors Hecate with a plate of food, some very dark wine, dark candles, an antique mirror, some cow bones, tree roots and a tiny spinning wheel. I lay out her feast and a feast for my ancestors, and I call her:

"Hail to You, Hecate, Queen of the Night, Queen of the Crossroad, Queen of all Witcheries and she who parts the Veil, we invite you to eat, drink and bide with us."

This can be followed by divination, meditation or scrying, but I find it offends her if I don't clean up her feast before I go to bed.

Leading up to Samhain, I try to do a "karmic accounting." I want to have my psychic and karmic debts paid before we head too deeply into the Dark of the Year. The darkening weeks after Samhain, as the year comes to an end and fall freezes into winter, are my time for a rigorous inventory of my life – am I doing what I should, what I dreamed of? Am I tending to my passions and responsibilities well?

Have I made good choices, and if not, what choices can I make now to correct my course? These can be dark times, with regrets and sorrows coming forward into the light of consciousness. Now is the time for the dark night of the soul, when the phantoms of our pain are so present. During November and December, Hecate appears to me with a compass, and with the roar of the ocean behind her, gales whipping foam off dark water, the crash of swells against black rock. This is Hecate as the soul of nature manifest in storms, hurricanes, tornados, earthquakes, lightning, thunder – all the forms that are dangerous to humans and therefore frightening. In every guise her silver eyes question me: What are you doing? Who are you? And I'm not always sure of the answers.

By Yule, nights have gotten cold and snowy, and incredibly dark. I love taking a walk on a winter night – it seems so incredibly forgiving and kind. It seems willing to help you with your burdens, to hold you in a starry embrace. I unbind my hair and let the wind whip through it, releasing what I don't need, clearing out my energetic body, breathing myself full of starlight. Hecate expands to take up the whole sky, the dark horizon. No longer slithering around dark corners or in the wild overgrown places next to trimmed lawns or orderly streets, Hecate is the immense, stellar darkness – the dark Earth, the cold sky, the gentle silence of snowy hills and icy clouds – receiving all, witnessing all, taking into Herself all that we release, with compassion and gentleness. I feel Her on Yule Eve in the role of Midwife to the Child of Light, encircling the energy of the Mother and Child in Her embrace, for all that is born into light must pass into shadow; Hecate bears witness to all the dramas of incarnation, with a face turned to each road, with her clear grey eye upon each potential.

In January, the Winter deepens into cold even as the light begins to grow. The cold drives me inside, and drives me deeper. I meditate longer, sit in contemplation more deeply. Information comes bubbling up to me during divination, but I can barely articulate what I find. Words become redundant, and I find myself silent for most of the day. The Year is in its infancy, and I'm learning what is to be my work for the year, what I'm supposed to and learn and experience, how I am to serve my Gods. In the cold silence, answers come that I must act upon, but cannot explain. Through dark woods, wolves lead me along hidden paths that never fail. She appears to me now in caves, brooding over her divinations as she sniffs out the business of the year. She is the bones of the world, the secrets of stone and strata and all the forces that build the earth up and tear it down. She is the wave wearing down stone, and mountains pushing their way up from the bottom of the sea. As I sit in contemplation, a chant comes to me:

Crone woman, stone woman
Claw shell bone woman
Lone woman alone woman
Dark mother star mother
Well river storm mother
Death Mother, Birth Mother
Earth Mother, Earth Mother.

By January 31, the light is appreciably stronger, the day longer. Imbolc is around the corner, and Hecate feels restive. She feels no love for the "fructifying Earth" as she calls the world in Springtime. She wants to retire to her dark cool places beneath the Earth. I have read that January 31 was one of her traditional feast days, and I have always felt her disappear after that day. I serve her traditional meal – fish – and pour dark wine and bring her dark chocolates and the darkest roses I can find. I wear wine colored velvet and light her candles, invite her to partake of the feast yet again.

I write out the work of the year, my dedications for the Imbolc flame and contemplate the waxing of the light. I scry with a black mirror, or with water in a tarnished silver bowl. Hecate slips into shadow and starlight, becomes mute and elusive. Before she departs I address her one more time: "Hecate, Queen of the Dead, of the Crossroad, of Choice and of Change and of the Mysterious, I thank you again for your presence in my life, for the lessons and blessings you have bestowed upon me, and for allowing me to serve you. As you retire to your secret places in the cool dark, I bid you farewell and await your return with the dying of the light." February 2 dawns and, fair or foul, I feel Demeter ending her mourning, beginning to smile, becoming again the gracious mother, warming us with her love. Soon it will be Spring and then Summer, and the Goddess of the Waxing Earth will be demanding my attention. But this evening is all Hecate's.

Hecate remains in the sweet dark places of my soul throughout the year, but in the heat of summer, she is very reclusive. I can find her if I look, but during these times I hold close the things she has taught me – to weigh my choices carefully, to speak truth, to be accountable, to have faith in the cycles of life and death and life again, and to hold myself a sovereign being in all dealings.

Pale Hekate

by Jacinta Cross

Pale Hekate has come to the garden
called by our pomegranate offering
beneath the shadowed hedge.
Her hands rake a trail of death,
dying in a spiral
bedded into the earth.

In her wake the mint sprigs emerge,
luscious and renewed.
Green children offering grace at the feet of death.

Flower of Fire: Hekate in the Chaldean Oracles

by Edward P. Butler

The *Chaldean Oracles*[1] is a revealed text attributed to Julian the Theurgist, a contemporary of the Emperor Marcus Aurelius (121-180 CE) and the son of another Julian, himself styled "the Chaldean." Whether 'Chaldean' here functions as an ethnic designation or refers to the career of astrologer is unknown; but there is little, if anything, to explicitly connect the *Oracles* to 'Chaldea'[2] (hence, whenever I use the term 'Chaldean' in this essay, it refers to the *Oracles*, and never to inhabitants of Mesopotamia). Though the *Chaldean Oracles* survive for us as an assemblage of fragments as evocative as they are obscure, the avid adoption of the *Oracles* into the canon of Late Antique pagan wisdom literature alongside much older texts and traditions speaks to their compelling appeal for those able to read them in their entirety. Due to the fragmentary state of their preservation, however, the modern literature on the *Oracles* has been dominated by efforts to resolve the problems of membership of fragments in the corpus, of their proper order, and, in short, of making the barest sense of what we possess of this influential text of Late Antiquity.

This effort has been further complicated by the necessity, for any understanding of the *Oracles*, of a fairly advanced understanding of the philosophical system of the Athenian Neoplatonists Proclus and Damascius, into which so much of what remains of the *Oracles* has been embedded; an understanding necessary as much in order to disentangle the *Oracles* from the exigencies of the Platonic system as to illuminate it from the latter. The curious interdisciplinary niche the *Oracles* occupied among these Neoplatonists has also hindered interpretation. Texts such as the Orphica were straightforwardly treated as 'theology', in the sense this term had for the Neoplatonists, that is, as a repository of information about the nature and functions of particular deities, but the *Oracles* seem to have been considered as theology and philosophy at once. We can see this from the Neoplatonists' appropriation of technical terminology from the *Oracles* for philosophical concepts; in particular the term *pêgê*, literally a spring or fountain, but used by Proclus especially to refer to intelligible (supra-intellectual) form. At the same time, the text was also treated like other 'theological' texts in comparative contexts, i.e., as expressing a particular configuration of divine persons. This dual status of the *Oracles* will be important to the present essay.

As a result of these factors, the effort of grasping what wisdom the *Oracles* may yet have to impart to us has really not even begun, nor is the very notion of such a project meaningful to those to whom, for their philological skills, the interpretation of the *Chaldean Oracles* has so far been entrusted. The present essay can barely make a beginning of this process, but hopefully can at least begin it in the proper way. To begin in the proper way means, in my judgment, to seek from the *Oracles* themselves rules for their interpretation. Such a rule is, I believe, offered in what has traditionally been considered fragment 1 of the corpus:

> For there exists a certain Intelligible which you must perceive by the flower of mind. For if you should incline your mind toward it and perceive it as perceiving a specific thing, you would not perceive it. For it is the power of strength, visible all around, flashing with intellectual divisions. Therefore, you must not perceive that Intelligible violently but with the flame of mind completely extended which measures all things, except that Intelligible. You must not perceive it intently, but keeping the pure eye of your soul turned away, you should extend an empty mind toward the Intelligible in order to comprehend it, since it exists outside of mind.[3]

The fragment states that there is 'something' intelligible (*ti noêton*) which cannot be intelligible *as something*, though it is "manifest on every side" (*amphiphaous*); that lies outside the totality or complete extension of the system in which all things are 'measured,' that is, against one another and according to common criteria, but 'flashes' with the application of such criteria (intellectual 'cuts', *tomai*); and that is the power (or possibility, *dunamis*) of 'strength' (*alkê*). Some of these aspects will be discussed more fully later in this essay; for now, however, I wish to concern myself specifically with the sense of 'something,' *ti*, here. The 'something' discussed in frag. 1 is very important; indeed, Majercik, in common with other commentators, sees in *ti noêton* "a reference to the highest God of the Chaldean hierarchy." But I believe that in so doing, Majercik and others violate the very hermeneutical condition set by the fragment itself, thus in fact foreclosing the possibility of making the *Oracles* themselves *operative*, by treating the 'something' as something distinct from the perceiving of it.[4] I propose that the fruitful way to understand 'something' here is not as a discrete something which comes to be known in a certain fashion, but instead as *whatever* comes to be known by the faculty designated here as "the flower of mind" (*nóou anthos*).

This 'something' – though it is not in a certain respect *something* at all – is indeed the first principle of the system of the *Chaldean Oracles*, and was known as the *hapax epekeina*, the 'single' or 'simplex' transcendent, as distinct from the *dis epekeina*, the 'double' or 'duplex' transcendent. It has been a commonplace to treat these as entities in a rather simplistic sense as the 'First God' and 'Second God' of the system, and indeed, when the former in particular is referred to repeatedly in the fragments as 'the Father,' it has seemed natural to personify them both. However, the author (likely Porphyry) of an anonymous commentary on Plato's *Parmenides*, states that "some" – by whom Pierre Hadot and Ruth Majercik both believe the author of the commentary intends the very author(s) of the *Oracles* – "see fit to abolish number" with respect to the 'Father' "in that they absolutely refuse even to say that he is *one*."[5]

There is no *one* identity for this figure, that is, it is not *numerically one*, because its identity is established simply as the object of the 'flower of mind,' whatever this faculty may be exercised upon, and thus primarily as a mode of being linked to a mode of cognition; and I believe that only in this fashion does the Chaldean 'Father' achieve a significance beyond the merely iconic. Thus Proclus states at *Platonic Theology* III 21. 74. 7-8 that "just as the intelligible Gods are henads[6] primarily, so too are they fathers primarily." This passage refers to his technical use of the term 'father' to characterize *a mode of divine activity*, a usage probably influenced by the *Chaldean Oracles*. Again, Proclus states in prop. 151 of his *Elements of Theology* that "All that is paternal in the Gods is of primal operation [*prôtourgon*] and stands in the position of the Good [*en tagathou taxei*] at the head of all the divine orders [*diakosmêseis*]."

If Proclus' remarks at 60K of his commentary on Plato's *Parmenides* about 'Ad' and 'Adad' indeed refer to lost material from the *Chaldean Oracles*, and thus identify the *dis epekeina* with the Syrian deity Hadad, with 'Ad' referring to the *hapax epekeina* as a back-formation, it still would not alter the fact that the primary reference of the *hapax* and *dis epekeina* is not to particular deities but to certain divine functions, viz. Majercik's remark that "this First God is generally described in Stoicizing terms as a primal, fiery Intellect...his nature is also regarded as essentially unknowable," (p. 138). A function, too, is 'essentially unknowable' as a particular nature because its nature is universal, that is, its nature is to be instantiated by whatever entities perform the function it defines, and to whatever degree they do so.

Identifications of the Chaldean functions with particular deities are possible, of course, especially with regard to the *dis epekeina*, e.g., Porphyry's identification of the *dis epekeina* with Yahweh (Lydus, *De mens.*, IV, 53), for the *Oracles* say with regard to the *dis epekeina* that "the Father perfected all things and handed them over to the Second, which you – the entire human race – call the First" (frag. 7), that is, because theologies accord to the foremost deity in their pantheon the absolute primacy that belongs, strictly speaking, to *each* deity in his/her perfect individuality.[7] Damascius states that the "universal demiurge" (that is, divinity operating as the intellectual structure of the cosmos)[8] has a sevenfold structure according to the Chaldeans, "each of them [the seven] being honored with the name of *dis epekeina* and containing in it all that the First does, only particularized in the declension into classes" (*De princ.* III 30. 13-16), elsewhere stating that the *dis epekeina* is divisible into a virtually unlimited plurality of intellects (*In Parm.* I 67. 24-5), or discrete cosmic operations.[9] Thus it is, in effect, the function of the duplex transcendent to 'measure' all things by dirempting or dividing itself to *become* the measures themselves.

But if the simplex and duplex transcendent are not, or are not only or primarily, discrete divine *entities*, but two modes of divine *activity*, the position of apparently the only *named* deity in the *Chaldean Oracles*,[10] and who is moreover explicitly presented as the divine operator of and the mediator between these two modes of activity, as we shall see, becomes even more important than has previously been appreciated; and that deity is none other than Hekate.

Hekate's name occurs in five fragments, she may be discussed in as many as 66 others, and she may be the speaker in as many as eleven fragments.[11] An especially important fragment relative to Hekate is frag. 50, which states that "the center [*kentron*] of Hekate is borne in the midst [*messon...pephorêsthai*] of the Fathers." Ontologically, this is interpreted, e.g., by Proclus (*In Tim.* II 129f) as the plane of psychical being, "as a medium between things that are intelligible only and things that are objects of sensation, between beings that are solely eternal, and those that are altogether generated." Hence Johnston, expressing a broad consensus among scholars of the *Oracles*, regards Hekate as simply equated with soul in the *Oracles*.[12] But this is unsatisfactory, as we shall see, inasmuch as the *Oracles*, while closely associating Hekate with the soul, do nevertheless distinguish them. Indeed, in Proclus' own interpretation of the Hellenic pantheon, the source of life for souls is seen more directly in Rhea, while the soul in its personal emergence is grasped through Persephone, who for Platonists embodies the soul's descent, not into death, but embodied life.[13] Hekate's special role in this process, I shall argue, is *revelatory*; and this is prefigured in her iconography, in which she typically bears twin torches.

G.R.S. Mead referred to the *Chaldean Oracles* as "The Gnosis of the Fire,"[14] and references to fire in them are too numerous to bother collecting here. One thing, though, may be stated in general about the sense of 'fire' in the *Oracles*: fire is never referred to there as consuming or destroying anything, and hence Chaldean 'fire' is clearly the "creative fire" (*pur technikon*) of the Stoic philosophers, which, unlike the fire which merely "converts fuel into itself," instead "causes growth and preservation, as is the case in plants and animals where it is natural constitution [*phusis*] and soul [*psuchê*]," (Zeno of Kition).[15] Chaldean 'fire,' then, is the very operative principle itself, actuality or activity (*energeia*). Frag. 6 states, probably of Hekate,[16] that "as a girdling, intellectual membrane" she "separates the first fire and the other fire which are eager to mingle," these fires generally being associated with the simplex and duplex transcendent. Hekate's iconic twin torches, though occasionally noted by modern commentators with regard to her characterization in the *Oracles* as *amphiphaês*, "shining on both sides" (frag. 189; cf. frag. 1, in which the intelligible object of the 'flower of mind' is described as *amphiphaous*, there translated by Majercik as "visible all around"), have not been sufficiently appreciated in interpreting her position between these two dispositions of 'fire', in part, I believe, because of the difficulty commentators have had in seeing these functions as her *instruments* rather than as divine *persons*. In this respect, Majercik's "reconsideration" regarding the commonplace among interpreters of a Chaldean 'divine triad' consisting of the *hapax epekeina*, Hekate, and the *dis epekeina* is salutary,[17] insofar as the tendency to treat this triad as a trinity of divine persons has distracted commentators from Hekate's dominant role as the sole named deity in the *Oracles*.

In frag. 6, Hekate is identified with an item of her equipment, her girdle (*zostêr*), in accord with a principle Damascius explains with respect to the processions of the Gods from their 'fontal' (*pêgaios*) being to their diversified 'principial' (*archikos*) activity. The "principial Hekate", e.g., emanates, he explains, from Hekate's crown, while "principial Soul" (*archikê psuchê*) and "principial Virtue" (*archikê aretê*) emanate from her girdle (*De princ.* III 38. 2-6), her adornments being the detachable counterparts, as it were, of her limbs, the girdle being analogous in this sense to her flanks (ibid. 39. 4-7). This refers to frags. 51 and 52 of the *Oracles*, which state that "In the left flank of Hekate exists the source of virtue [or 'fontal virtue', *aretês pêgê*], which remains entirely within and does not give up its virginity," (52) while "Around the hollow of her right flank a great stream of the primordially-generated Soul gushes forth in abundance, totally ensouling light, fire, ether, worlds," (51). Proclus alludes to these fragments in his commentary on Plato's *Timaeus* regarding the opposed circular motions of the soul, the "circles of sameness and difference" of *Timaeus* 36c, implying that Hekate's 'girdle' may be taken as these motions (*In Tim.* II 260.28-261.3). Whereas the account in the *Timaeus*, however, is of simple circular motions, the descriptions of the emanations from Hekate, if they are to be harmonized with the Platonic text, would suggest one motion spiraling outward – and perhaps the use of *peri*, 'about', already indicates something other than a simple outward streaming – while the other cannot be literally stationary but must be either a circular motion or a complementary spiraling inward, that is, centrifugal and centripetal motion, ensouling with the centrifugal and establishing virtue or perfecting the soul with the centripetal.

The significance to ancient physics of the vortex and other concepts from fluid dynamics has been argued by Michel Serres with particular reference to ancient atomism.[18] Serres has an innovative reading of atomism that focuses on the role of what he calls the "system of turbulence."[19] Serres' reading assimilates atoms to vortices in fluids, similar in certain respects to William Thomson's 19th century theory of atoms as "loci of a special type of rotary motion within a homogeneous aether pervading space," with the consequence that matter is properly understood as "a mode of motion."[20] The fragments of the *Chaldean Oracles* abound with vivid references to fluid and turbulent motion. In the *Oracles*, the "life-giving" fire "furrows" (36) and "rolls up" (38) into "channels" (60, 65, 66, 75, 110, 189); air, too, is described in terms of "streams," "hollows" and "channels" (61); and one of the forms of theophany is "a sumptuous light, rushing like a spiral" (146). Indeed, it seems that there is a common language of fluid turbulence applied on all planes of being: "All things serve these three turbulent rulers/principles [*archais labrois*]," namely the "sacred course [*hieros dromos*]," the course of air, and the third, "which heats the earth by fire" (73). A common dynamics is also implied in the concept of diverse "ethers" belonging to each of the elements (62, 98) but presumably exhibiting similar turbulence activity. Within this differentiated fluid medium the "intelligible Thoughts from the Paternal Source" are said to "break" like waves upon "the bodies of the worlds," "borne around the sublime wombs like a swarm of bees" (37),[21] the Sources and Principles (*pêgai* and *archai*) are "whirled about in ceaseless motion" (49), as the "seven firmaments of the worlds" are "inflated" (57).

Within this dynamic context, Hekate, borne along in the midst of the 'Fathers' as if in a sea constituted by primary divine activity, establishes of and for herself a "center" (50), a center which clearly must be the result of an active *centering* in relative motion, as Damascius comments on frag. 50: "in terms of center she [Hekate] is in repose, but in terms of being carried she is moved," (*In Parm.* III 60.1-4). I attribute this centering specifically to the contrary (centrifugal/centripetal) motions of/from Hekate in frs. 51 and 52, which are also, and crucially, activities on behalf of the soul. I will consider further below the significance of the contrariety of these motions; but first I wish to discuss the elemental motion I believe to be common to the two.

The enigmatic frag. 63 tells us that "a single [or 'unique,' *mian*] line is drawn in a curved shape," upon which Damascius comments (*In Parm.* II 101.10-11) that the *Oracles* "make a great use of linear shape" (*tou grammiaiou schêmatos*). The term for 'drawn' here, *suromenê*, is also used in frag. 34, which states, regarding "the birth of variegated matter," that from the "Source of Sources" (*pêgê pêgôn*) "a lightning-bolt, sweeping along (*suromenos*), obscures the flower of fire as it leaps into the hollows of the worlds," while frag. 164 speaks of a precipice beneath the earth "drawing [*surôn*]" something – perhaps the soul, or simply exerting a 'draw' – "down from the threshold with seven paths [*kata heptaporou bathmidos*],"[22] and frag. 70 speaks of the heaven (*ouranos*), ruled by "untiring Nature" which is in turn "suspended from the great Hekate," "pulling down [*katasurôn*] its eternal course," implying a constant downdraft motion like the atomists' eternal cascade (or "laminar flow," in Serres' term) of atoms, with turbulence supplied by the curving line corresponding to the atomic 'swerve' or oblique motion, *parenklisis* in Greek or *clinamen* in Latin, a minimal indeterminacy or unpredictability that introduces "creative chaos" into the parallel flows of atoms falling in the infinite void, and spontaneity into the otherwise deterministic universe.[23] The atomic swerve is thus the turbulence minimum as well as the minimum nonzero value for a curve, the line in Euclidean geometry being a 'straight curve', and it is this swerve I wish to argue underlies both of the motions attributed to the Chaldean Hekate.

This indeterminate or turbulent motion, which can be expressed by the minimum curve and symbolized by the spiral, pertains especially to Chaldean Hekate because of her association with the instrument known as 'Hekate's top' or 'magic wheel' (*strophalon*), mentioned in frag. 206, but more properly known as an *iynx* (whence the English word 'jinx'), which gives its name to an important species of divine entity in the Chaldean system, the Iynges.[24] Frag. 37 characterizes the Platonic Ideas as "whirring forth" (*erroizêse*) from the Paternal Intellect in similitude to such whirling tops, and Damascius states that "The Great Hekate sends forth a lifegiving whir [*zôogonon rhoizêma*]," (*In Parm.* III 42.16-8). The whirling motion of the daimonic Iynges is conceived as a form of self-motion: the Iynges "which are thought paternally [*patrothen noeousi*] also think themselves, since they are moved by unspeakable counsels [*boulais aphthenktois*] so as to think," (frag. 77).[25] To grasp this statement operatively, we must understand the state of being 'paternally thought' as *identical* to the state of being 'moved by unspeakable counsels,' and both as being identical to the whirling or helical motion itself.

The 'counsels' or directions according to which the Iynges are moved are not unspeakable as the result of some arbitrary prohibition; rather, they are unspeakable because it is impossible to express *in advance* the value or course of the swerve. Here Chaldean 'ineffability' and atomistic indeterminacy converge. Under the conditions of a system "in which the initial conditions determining various qualitatively distinct behaviors are not clearly separated but are, on the contrary, as close as one might wish,"

> in order to predict deterministically the type of behavior the system will adopt, one would need *infinite* precision. It is of no use to increase the level of precision or even to make it *tend* toward infinity; uncertainty always remains complete – it does not diminish as precision increases. That means that divine knowledge is no longer implied in human knowledge as its limit, as that toward which one might tend with increasing precision; it is something other, separated by a gap.[26]

It is not a matter here, however, of some arcane 'higher' knowledge, but of the transition between knowledge as such and living volition. To be 'paternally thought/moved' is to be *self thought/moved*, for to be 'paternally thought' is to be an object of thought in a manner that transcends intellection itself; it is to be a unique, spontaneous and, in the physicist's terms, "irreversible" individual. The *gap* representing such individuals in the intellectual system or economy is expressed in the *Oracles* by discontinuous motions like 'leaping' and 'flashing,' especially as of lightning (e.g., frags. 1, 34, 35, 37, 42, 76, 87, 90, 147, 148, 190) and less often, by 'abysses' (e.g., frags. 112, 183, 184, but in particular frag. 18: "You who know the hypercosmic paternal abyss by perceiving it").[27]

I have elsewhere argued for the reciprocal implication of the 'paternal' mode of activity and metaphysical individuality in Proclus;[28] what we see in the *Oracles* may lie at the root of this peculiar doctrine, at least in the terms in which Proclus chooses to express it. Damascius emphasizes that the line drawn into a curve is 'one,' possibly with the sense 'unique' – a unique curving trajectory for *each* self-moving helical 'fire'. Damascius makes special reference to the spiral or helix just before he cites frag. 63, explaining that (commenting on Plato, *Parmenides* 145b1-5) a 'figure' or 'shape' (*schêma*) is to be conceived in general as "that which is inscribed in an angle, even if it is not closed," and hence "the spiral [*helix*] is a shape for us, as in theology," the latter probably a reference to the *Oracles* (*In Parm.* II 100.22-101.2), since frag. 146 describes the theophany of an unidentified deity as being accompanied by a light "rushing like a spiral [*rhoizaion helichthen*]." But earlier in the discussion Damascius refers to theology in a more theoretical sense, when treating the supra-intellectual character of shape, which he conceives as the "autocircumscription of a substance" (*tês ousias autoperigraphos*). Inasmuch as intellect, too, is self-circumscribing, for it converges upon itself, intellect possesses 'shape' and therefore shape is metaphysically prior to intellect. Accordingly, "the determination [*aphorismos*] of shapes is theological," (ibid., p. 100.20-21), because in the Neoplatonic hierarchical ontology, the theological is prior to being (the ontological) and hence to intellect.[29] Shapes demonstrate their supra-intellectual character through, for example, the presence in them of irrational numbers and infinite quanta; but shape is theological for Damascius also, and indeed especially, insofar as shapes are the *self*-circumscription of substances, and thus share in the intrinsic selfhood of that which is prior to formal (universal, intellectual) being.

The soteriological framework of the *Chaldean Oracles*, however, urges us to augment the static reading with a dynamic one that emphasizes, not the ontological position of individuals, but their power to change their state, which begins, for the *Oracles*, from the very material ground of manifestation. "Primordial matter," states frag. 173, "is starry and heavenly;" hence "if you extend your mind, illumined by fire, to the work of piety," one may "save the flowing body" as well (frag. 128), while frag. 97 urges us to "boast of the harmony under which the mortal body exists," and frag. 129 to "save also the mortal covering of bitter matter." It is unnecessary to engage in the debates over whether Chaldean salvation amounts to saving the body from its infirmities, or a corporeal resurrection, or saving only the vehicle of the soul, and not the flesh; what matters is that whatever they do, the means of doing it lies in the *Oracles'* fluid-dynamic account of ideality, which establishes a common plane of intellectual and material process.

As a result of their inexpressible (self-)guidance, the *iynges* are essentially free themselves, but they can be a source of bondage in other things. Frag. 223 speaks of entities that are drawn "unwilling from the ether by means of unspeakable [*aporrêtois*] *iynges*," and the presence of *iynx*-wheels in the hands of *erotes* in art of the classical and Hellenistic periods shows that these self-moving or ineffably guided entities are most readily perceived in passionate complexes with the power to *subvert* the will.[30] Such complexes are in effect *partial souls* themselves. Thus every soul must secure its own freedom in a turbulent cosmos full of binding and liberating forces, both of which have their origin in the elemental 'freedom' of the swerve-motion.[31]

With this consideration the perspective of our inquiry begins to shift, in effect, from the 'torch' of ensouling or vivification to the 'torch' of perfecting or virtue. The essence of virtue in the *Oracles* is, effectively, liberation, especially from binding forces like the "chthonian dogs" referred to in frag. 90, who "leap from the hollows of the earth" and "never show a true sign to mortals," while frag. 91 speaks of a female "driver of dogs of the air, earth, and water," perhaps meaning Hekate. These feral forces are probably the same as the "earthly beasts [*thêres chthonos*]" that frag. 157 warns can "occupy your vessel." There should be nothing surprising in Hekate's control over binding and liberating forces alike, for everything that lives does so by binding certain things to itself and separating itself from other things. There is hence nothing evil or vengeful about the actions of these 'dogs', who occupy a niche in a natural order in which souls unable to secure their integrity are subject to attack from forces seeking to bind their substance to their own. Indeed, it is beneficent that such forces should be under Hekate's control, because she can always lead a soul out of whatever bondage it has acquired.

Frag. 125 states that the duplex transcendent sows in the worlds "lights which are set free," and Proclus states in his fragmentary commentary on the *Chaldean Oracles* that "every life [*zôê*]" possesses "its own easily liberated [*euluton*] energy," (*De phil. Chald.* 2). Understanding that the forms of bondage are many, what techniques for liberation do the *Oracles* impart? Frag. 124 speaks of "those who, by inhaling, thrust out [*exôstêres*] the soul"[32] and hence "are free". This simultaneous drawing in and pushing out recalls the centrifugal and centripetal motions around Hekate, and expresses the soul's stabilizing or 'centering' itself in the cosmos. On the one hand, the soul draws 'inspiration', so to speak, from the "symbols" that "the Paternal Intellect has sown ... throughout the cosmos, (the Intellect) which thinks the intelligibles. And (these intelligibles) are called inexpressible beauties," (frag. 108). The symbols sown by the Paternal Intellect, in accord with the nature of the 'paternal' plane of action, are significant *relative to each unique individual*; hence they act through the experience of beauty, the most subjective of perceptions, in this way illuminating a path specific to each soul. As Damascius explains in the discussion incorporating frag. 1 of the *Oracles*, the ground of intelligibility may not lie in an object's presenting itself to the intellect "as an object of cognition [*gnôston*], but as an object of desire [*epheton*]," so that the intellect's striving is fulfilled "not by knowledge [*gnôsis*] but by substance [*ousia*] and by the total and intelligible perfection," (*De princ.* II 104. 20-23).

The striving for knowledge fulfills itself at last in the object of desire that perfects, not merely the mind, but the *whole* being, whether

149

we are speaking about the mind of a mortal creature or the 'mind' of the cosmos itself, that is, its own tendency to order and to higher states of complexity. For this reason Proclus augments the *Oracles'* concept of the "flower of the intellect" with that of the "flower of the whole soul" which serves to unite the individual with the One, that is, with their own absolute individuality, on the basis of the recovery of which, and only on this basis, is it possible to obtain direct experience of one's patron or tutelary deity, according to the principle that like knows like: "as we apprehend intellect by becoming intellectually-formed [*noeideis*], so becoming unit-formed [*henoeideis*] we ascend to unity [*henosis*]," (*De phil. Chald.* 4). It is not a matter here of 'uniformity', but of *individuation*, nor of dissolving into the deity, but of authentic theophany, one-on-one. This is what it means to *apprehend by unity*, unique individual to unique individual. In this encounter the totality self-perceives, for the totality is comprised in the unique, since only an infinite determination is unrepeatable.

Proclus explains that in "celebrating divine things" the soul is perfected by "placing before and carrying to the Father the ineffable symbols of the Father, which the Father placed in the soul in the first progression of essence [*ousias*]," (*De phil. Chald.* 1; trans. T. M. Johnson). Individual souls, by completing their substance through striving for the things that are beautiful to them, return to the God (or Goddess) they worship something that has proceeded primordially from that God: "the Paternal Intellect does not receive the will [*thelein*] of <the soul> until <the soul> emerges from forgetfulness and speaks a word, remembering the pure, paternal token," (frag. 109). This token is 'paternal' by virtue of its peculiarity to the individual in question; and by "remembering" it and its origin in the divine beauty, the individual is incorporated into the self-understanding of the God, and insofar as this is a moment in the existential individuality of the Gods themselves, the worshiper participates in the 'paternal' activity of the divine. Proclus explains that the "flower of the intellect", though "intellectual...is apprehended by the Paternal Intellect according to the unity [*hen*] in it," (*De phil. Chald.* 4) for in the flower of intellect what the Gods recognize is not primarily intellectual content, but rather our very individuality expressed through it. This is why, as frag. 13 states, "nothing imperfect [*ateles*] runs forth from the Paternal Principle," for on the plane of 'paternal' activity, there is no *telos*, no end separable even in principle from each individual who is ontologically an end in itself. In this regard, a Stoic pun on the name of Hekate may be instructive: 'Hekate' is so called *dia to hekastou pronoeisthai*, "on account of <her> foreknowledge of <or 'providence' for> *each* [*hekastos*]."[33]

The duplex transcendent, on the other hand, involves self-reflection or self-objectivation, and thus is a "dyad" or double (Proclus,

In Crat. 51.18-52.3). Hence frag. 5 states that "the craftsman of the fiery cosmos" is "intellect <derived> from intellect [*nou nóos*]." In more abstract terms, Damascius, using Chaldean terminology to speak about Platonic concepts, calls the demiurge (i.e., the duplex transcendent) "twice the simplex" and the infra-intellectual processions of the Gods as "twice the duplex" (*In Parm.* II 132.4-5), because the act of self-reflection essential to demiurgic intelligence, as Proclus explains, quoting the *Oracles*, "has a double function: it both possesses the intelligibles in its mind and brings sense-perception to the worlds," (frag. 8; ibid., 51.29-30). The knowledge possessed in and through the duplex transcendent is *objective* knowledge in a very special sense, namely that in its awareness of possessing thought it *is* the very objectivity of its contents, which results, in a further evolution of the divine activity, in a squaring, so to speak, of the state of duplex transcendency into a mode of activity that is "twice the twice" and identical with *aisthêsis,* or sense-perception, the plane of activity of the encosmic divine processions. In similar fashion, frag. 25 states that "the Father thought these things and a mortal was brought to life by him," that is, a mortal *qua* mortal, *ateles,* for its *telos* is thought separately from it. This progression of modes of intelligence, from the "partless, simple, and indivisible" simplex transcendency (frag. 152), to the objectifying self-analysis of duplex transcendency, which allows it to unfold from a dyad, to a triad (frags. 27-9), or a tetrad, or a hebdomad, or the unlimited multiplicity (i.e., infinite divisibility) inherent in sense-perception, and back again, is the cycle of manifestation in the *Oracles.*

I have spoken of Hekate's torches, but another element of her traditional equipment seems to have been incorporated into the Chaldean system, namely her *keys.*[34] For Damascius says, regarding the intelligible intellect (or "all-perfect animal(ity)", *zôion panteles*) of the Platonists and the third intelligible-intellective triad, the "perfective" (*telesiourgos*) plane of divine activity, that "the one and the other are celebrated as 'keys' by the Gods themselves" (frag. 197; *In Parm.* II 99. 11-12), attribution simply to 'the Gods' being a common shorthand way of referring to a provenance from the *Oracles.* It is impossible to say just how Damascius arrives at such a precise identification between elements of the highly articulated Platonic system and the *Oracles,* but it would be prudent to assume that this precision means we are dealing with functions distinct from the simplex and duplex transcendency as such, though obviously related to them. These keys, I believe, insofar as we may understand them through their philosophical elaboration, are the *virtues* corresponding to the two fires. Virtue itself, we recall, emanates from Hekate's left side (frag. 52), but it has a dual aspect, just as we could regard the centrifugal and centripetal motions as in effect two aspects of ensouling, which emanated from her right (frag. 51).

The two primary Chaldean virtues, that is, those with a cosmogonic function, are *love* and *strength*. Frag. 39 explains that "after he thought his works, the self-generated Paternal Intellect sowed the bond of Love, heavy with fire, into all things...in order that the All might continue to love for an infinite time and the things woven by the intellectual light of the Father might not collapse...with this Love, the elements of the world remain on course." The concern that things not "collapse" seems akin to what is said in frag. 68, that the 'maker' (*poiêtês*) fashioned things so that "the world might be manifest [*ekdêlos*] and not seem membrane-like [*humenôdês*]." At the same time, frag. 104 warns us not to "deepen the surface [*bathunês toupipedon*]." Plainly there are conflicting orientations at work, one which *deepens* – cf. frag. 183, "the real is in the depth [*en bathei*]" – where the other *flattens*. With the motion of deepening go the references to *extension* (various forms of *teinai*) as in frags. 1 and 128, which refer to "extending" the mind, an activity grounded in the duplex transcendent, for frag. 12 states that "the Monad is extensible [*tanaê*] which generates duality." In extending itself the mind generally "measures" things (frag. 1), that is, it relates things to one another and associates them in the understanding, thus 'deepening' the world through its 'supports' – for "every world possesses unbending intellectual supports" (frag. 79) – but when the mind is extended to the simplex transcendent it has the effect instead of *flattening* these supports and opening up 'channels' of turbulence (association?) across the planes that are ordinarily distinct. In this way we "perceive the shape of light which has been stretched forth [*protatheisan*]," (frag. 145) in the world's "inflation" (frag. 57).

But this 'flattening' is not like seeing through an illusion; instead, it is what prevents the 'paternal' works from 'collapse', because it liberates the creative fire which is in the control of all self-moving beings. Thus frag. 42 speaks of Love "which leapt first from Intellect, clothing his fire with the bonded [*sundesmion*] fire in order to mingle the fontal cups [*pêgaious kratêras*] while offering the flower of his fire."[35] These "fontal cups" or "source kraters" are pre-intellectual forms "mingled" or rearranged in the "bonds" created by worldly entities when they take up their agency in recognition of one another. Hence the soul is said to be filled "with a deep love [*erôti bathei*]" (frag. 43), because in forming bonds it creates new 'depths', which are at once worldly supports and counterworldly abysses. This movement of *eros* is, I believe, the "thrusting forth" of the soul that frag. 124 described as simultaneous with 'inhaling' or 'inspiration' in those who are "free."

This is the Chaldean virtue of love; as for the other 'key', the virtue of strength, we read in frag. 1 that the object of the 'flower of mind' is the *dunamis alkês*, which Majercik translates, rather redundantly, as "the power of strength". To avoid the redundancy, we can read *dunamis* instead as 'potentiality' or 'possibility', and understand the simplex transcendent as the precondition for that which the *Oracles* term 'strength'. Frags. 49 speaks of "the strength of the Father" from which "the flower of the mind" is "plucked" so as to keep the Sources and Principles (*pêgai* and *archai*) "whirling about in ceaseless motion;" frag. 82 explains that this strength infuses the 'Connectors', *sunocheis*, Gods presiding over the establishment of the transverse planes or 'channels' I have characterized as being produced through the 'flattening' motion. 'Strength', then, is what maintains motion and keeps the diverse planes of action in communication, and it is peculiarly associated with the *possession of a symbol* or revelation. Frag. 118 explains that "some apprehend the symbol of light through instruction" while others are "fructified with their own strength while they are sleeping," that is, through receiving dream symbols; frag. 117, likewise, speaks of those "saved through their own strength," who are characterized by Proclus as the more "vigorous" and "inventive" natures (*In Alc.* 82/177), while frag. 2 urges one "arrayed from head to toe with a clamorous light, armed in mind and soul with a triple-barbed strength" to "go toward the empyrean channels...with concentration," by "casting into your imagination the entire token of the triad." The "triad" in question is none other than the "triple-barbed strength" granted by possession of a "token," *sunthêma*, a personal, we might even say *idiosyncratic* revelation that arms the theurgist for the cosmogonic work demanded of them. It is a triad because, as frag. 27 states, "in every world shines a triad, ruled by a Monad," for this is the elemental structure of manifestation, the triangle being the minimum *enclosed* figure, as opposed to the spiral, the minimal 'open' figure in the Chaldean system according to Damascius. Armed with this token, the theurgist is charged, literally, with reinventing the world.

Conclusion

When we reach out with the flower of mind and recognize the uniqueness of things, the Gods reach back to us through the flower of the entire soul, which is "the whole essence of the center and of all the diverse powers around it," the unity "upon which all the psychical powers converge," which "alone naturally leads us to that which is beyond all beings," (*De phil. Chald.* 4). This systole and diastole of enlightenment is Hekate's work, for she performs in and from herself the centrifugal motion of vivification, the primary procession from the simplex transcendent, which is freedom with the power to bind, and the centripetal motion of perfection, the return of the 'bound' intellectual and symbolic structure of the cosmos to its free and erotic origins, which is liberation through the duplex transcendent. By virtue of these reciprocal motions, Hekate is responsible for the soul's dynamical centering on the 'paternal' plane of primary, or individuating, activity.

Excursus: Hekate in the *Homeric Hymn to Demeter*

The activities of the Chaldean Hekate can be understood as an intensive meditation upon and elaboration of Hekate's actions in the *Homeric Hymn to Demeter*, which fall into three stages:

1. (*HHD* 22-5): Hekate, described as "Perses' daughter still innocent of heart [*atala phroneousa*]," hears Persephone's cries "from her cave [*ex antrou*]," as does Helios.

Here, Hekate is quiescent, but responds to the "voice" of the soul descending to embodiment, to which compare the "lifegiving whir" or "hum" (*rhoizêma*) with which Damascius associates Hekate (*In Parm.* III 42.18).

2. (51-61): On the tenth day [*dekatê*] of her search, Demeter meets Hekate "with a light in her hand [*selas en cheiressin echousa*]" and tells her what she heard. Demeter runs with her "with burning torches in her hands" to Helios, who saw the events.

The numbers *ten* and *four* (the ten being the expansion of four, 1+2+3+4) are spoken of as "key-bearers", *kleidouchoi* in the pseudo-Iamblichean *Theology of Arithmetic* (28.13, 81.14 de Falco), this being an epithet of Hekate's as well. The text refers first to Hekate's single light at first, but then to Demeter's twin torches, as they run back to Helios to retrieve the vision. Thus, at the furthest limits of the centrifugal motion, the centripetal motion of "virtue" (keys) comes into play.

3. (438-440): Hekate, described as at 25 as "of the glossy veil [*liparokrêdemnos*]," embraces Persephone on her return, and "the mistress [*anassa*]" becomes Persephone's attendant and servant [*propolos kai opaôn*].

At the beginning and the end of the sequence, Hekate is veiled, as when the world is rendered flat or "membrane-like [*humenôdês*]" (frag. 68). In embracing Persephone on her return, that is, the soul upon its liberation from self-imposed bondage, Hekate is acknowledged as Mistress, and assumes a role of guide and helper to the soul in its future transformations ("ascents" and "descents").

¹ Throughout this essay I shall use the simpler spelling 'Chaldean' rather than 'Chaldaean', more correct but slightly off-putting to the English reader's eye.

² See, however, Polymnia Athanassiadi, "Apamea and the *Chaldaean Oracles* : A Holy City and a Holy Book," in *The Philosopher and Society in Late Antiquity : Essays in Honour of Peter Brown*, ed. Andrew Smith (Swansea: Classical Press of Wales, 2005), pp. 117-143, which argues for a link between the *Oracles* and the temple of Bel in Apamea, which had a tradition of oracular production as well as a thriving Hellenistic philosophical culture.

³ Unless otherwise noted, all translations of Oracle fragments are by Ruth Majercik, *The Chaldean Oracles: Text, Translation, and Commentary* (Leiden: E. J. Brill, 1989).

⁴ Cf. frag. 20, "For Intellect does not exist without the intelligible, and the intelligible does not exist apart from Intellect."

⁵ Ruth Majercik, "Chaldean Triads in Neoplatonic Exegesis: Some Reconsiderations," *The Classical Quarterly*, Vol. 51, No. 1 (2001), p. 266f (on the identity of the "some" referred to here, see also Majercik, "The *Chaldean Oracles* and the School of Plotinus," *The Ancient World* Vol. 29 (1998), 103f, with refs. to Hadot, n. 80). Majercik interprets the abolition of number here as coming about purely through the identification of the Chaldean 'Father' with the Platonic One, which *is not one*; I would claim rather that there is a convergence here between Platonic doctrine and a doctrine legitimately deriving from the *Oracles*—which is not inconsistent with its presence there being due to the influence of earlier Platonic speculation, especially that concerning the characterization of the Platonic demiurge as 'maker and father' of the cosmic order at *Timaeus* 28c.

⁶ 'Henads': existentially unique individuals. For Proclus' doctrine of henads, see my article "Polytheism and Individuality in the Henadic Manifold," *Dionysius*, Vol. 23, 2005, pp. 83-103. On the 'Intelligible Gods' specifically, see "The Intelligible Gods in the *Platonic Theology* of Proclus," *Méthexis* 21, 2008, pp. 131-143.

⁷ On these matters, see my "Polycentric Polytheism and the Philosophy of Religion," *The Pomegranate* 10.2 (2008), esp. pp. 222ff.

⁸ On the nature of the Platonic demiurge, see Eric Perl, "The Demiurge and the Forms: A Return to the Ancient Interpretation of Plato's *Timaeus*," *Ancient Philosophy* 18 (1998), pp. 81-92.

⁹ Citations of Damascius are to volume, page and line number of *Damascius: Traité des premiers principes*, ed. L. G. Westerink and trans. Joseph Combès, 3 vols. (Paris: Les Belles Lettres, 1986-1991) [*De princ.*], and *Damascius: Commentaire du Parménide de Platon*, ed. L. G. Westerink and trans. J. Combès, with the collaboration of A.-P. Segonds, 4 vols. (Paris: Les Belles Lettres, 1997-2003) [*In Parm.*].

10 Either Rhea's appearance in frag. 56, or the fragment's membership in the corpus, is controversial (see Majercik, p. 165 and "Chaldean Triads", p. 291-4), and the connection of Atlas to frag. 6 doubtful. Zeus appears in frs. 215 and 218, but neither of these are likely to belong to the *Oracles*.

11 Reckoning according to Sarah Iles Johnston, *Hekate Soteira: A Study of Hekate's Roles in the Chaldean Oracles and Related Literature* (Atlanta: Scholars Press, 1990), 1f.

12 Johnston, *Hekate Soteira*, pp. 153-163.

13 For the Platonic interpretation of Persephone, see Thomas Taylor, *A Dissertation on the Eleusinian and Bacchic Mysteries* (1790). For Hekate's role in the *Homeric Hymn to Demeter*, see the Excursus at the end of this essay.

14 *The Chaldaean Oracles* (*Echoes from the Gnosis* Vol. VIII), p. 20.

15 Stobaeus 1.213, 15-21 (*SVF* 1.120; Long & Sedley, *Hellenistic Philosophers*, 46D).

16 This being the judgment of Majercik (p. 143) and Johnston (*Hekate Soteira*, p. 53). Simplicius quotes this fragment with reference to Atlas, but this seems to be a comparison rather than an identification.

17 "Chaldean Triads in Neoplatonic Exegesis: Some Reconsiderations", esp. pp. 286-296.

18 For an introduction to Serres' work in English, see the essays in *Hermes: Literature, Science, Philosophy*, ed. Josué V. Harari and David F. Bell (Baltimore: Johns Hopkins Univ. Press, 1982).

19 Michel Serres and Bruno Latour, *Conversations on Science, Culture, and Time*, trans. Roxanne Lapidus (Ann Arbor: Univ. of Michigan Press, 1995), p. 54.

20 Robert H. Silliman, "William Thomson: Smoke Rings and Nineteenth-Century Atomism," *Isis*, Vol. 54, No. 4 (Dec., 1963), p. 461.

21 Trans. mod.

22 Trans. mod.

23 See Ilya Prigogine's and Isabelle Stengers' "Postface: Dynamics from Leibniz to Lucretius," pp. 137-155 in *Hermes*, op cit.

24 On the *iynx* in relation to the *Oracles*, see Chap. VII in Johnston, *Hekate Soteira*; for the general use of this and similar instruments in ancient magic, see A. S. F. Gow, "*Iygx, Rombos, Rhombus, Turbo*," *Journal of Hellenic Studies*, Vol. 54, Part 1 (1934), pp. 1-13.

25 Trans. mod.

26 Prigogine and Stengers, op cit., 151f. Contrast this with Lewy, *The Chaldean Oracles and Theurgy*, who attributes to Hekate two *different* sorts of motion: "In the region of the stars … the action of 'ensouling' produces regular motion, which in the absence of a contrary force bears the character of pure necessity," while in the "hylic world", "where Spirit is opposed to Matter … the demonic satellites of the latter are active," (p. 98). In my interpretation, 'free' motion is characteristic of Hekate's activity both on the 'higher' and the 'lower' planes.

[27] Note also, with respect to the parallels I have drawn here between the *Oracles* and ancient atomism, that frag. 183, "the real is in the depth [*to d'atrekes en bathei esti*]" virtually quotes verbatim Democritus, frag. 117 (Diels), "for truth is in the depths [*en buthôi gar hê alêtheia*]".

[28] See "The Intelligible Gods in the *Platonic Theology* of Proclus."

[29] The hypostasis of Being is functionally duplex insofar as it is passive with respect to the Gods, who are prior to it, active with respect to Intellect, which is posterior to it. In this regard it is not uncommon, since Being is the first genuine hypostasis—the One neither is, nor is one—to split Being into its divine and intellectual moments. Thus Proclus explains at *PT* III 21. 74f the equivocations by means of which "Plato himself and his most genuine disciples frequently call all [true] beings intellect," while the henads or Gods "are frequently called intelligibles," as the ultimate causes of intellectual structure, "and beings are called intelligible intellects," as structures accessible to intellectual analysis. For more on the status of Being, see my "The Gods and Being in Proclus," *Dionysius*, Vol. 26, 2008, pp. 93-114.

[30] See Sarah Iles Johnston, "The Song of the *Iynx*: Magic and Rhetoric in *Pythian* 4," *Transactions of the American Philological Association*, Vol. 125 (1995), pp. 177-206.

[31] Cf. the still unsurpassed account by Giordano Bruno in his 1588 essay *De Vinculis in genere* ("A General Account of Bonding"), trans. Richard J. Blackwell in *Cause, Principle and Unity and Essays on Magic* (Cambridge: Cambridge University Press, 1998), pp. 143-176.

[32] Trans. mod.

[33] *SVF* II 930.

[34] On Hekate as *kleidouchos*, or "keybearer", see Johnston, *Hekate Soteira*, pp. 39-48.

[35] Trans. mod.

Prayer to Hekate

by Rebecca Buchanan

Hekate
Dark Serpent
Who feasts on the dead
      the rotten
      the fetid
Feast on me
Feast on all that is putrid in me
      the crippling fear
      the destructive anger
      the hatred of self and others
Make me new again
      pure
      like the snake
      reborn

(After a hymn to Hekate in the Greek Magical Papyri)

Artemesia shivered and wished that she had brought the other wrap with her, the thick woolen one that her mother wove for her as a present on her wedding day. It was gaily colored, dyed a rich purple-red, and it had strong associations that didn't seem appropriate for what she had come to this place to do tonight. Instead she chose the simple white linen one that reminded her of a corpse's burial shroud, and she shivered in the chill Alexandrian night.

Even though she'd been in the city for several years now, she still wasn't used to the difference in temperature. She'd been born in Antinoopolis, in the heart of the Egyptian countryside, far from the Mediterranean and its cool trade winds. Alexandria might as well have been a different country altogether, and the weather was only one of the jarringly different things about it. There were also the people – a million of them, crowding the streets by day and celebrating all through the night. It seemed that they never slept, these riotous, lecherous, drunken people from a hundred different countries. At all hours you could hear them hawking their wares down by the dock-side or staggering home from a party with a broken garland-crown around their neck and some wine-sotted bawdy song upon their lips. Half the time you couldn't even tell what they were singing: Greek vied with Latin or Aramaic or some other barbarous tongue from a foreign boat docked in the harbor. Of course you didn't need to know what language they spoke when they stopped you on the street and made lewd advances as if you were some wanton whore for hire, even when you were far from the district where Aphrodite's daughters congregated.

Artemesia hated it here and longed for home. Antinoopolis was a large city, but nothing was as large as this place, except perhaps for Rome. Everyone here was a stranger, even people who lived in the same tiny rooming-house. Everyone hated each other too: she was constantly overhearing her neighbors' shrill voices as they screamed at each other or broke things. Usually, a couple hours later, she'd hear the equally angry, desperate sounds of their lovemaking.

She wondered if that's what she and Sarapion sounded like to them. They had had plenty of nasty fights since moving here, and mended their broken hearts plenty of times with that mindless, animalistic sex afterwards. Of course, lately, there had mostly just been the fighting. Sarapion had grown cold and distant with her. He no longer kissed her or called her sweet pet names. He looked at her with empty, bored eyes and the only things he had to say to her were minor criticisms of her cooking and housework. Even these had become infrequent, and when she questioned him about their marriage and what she could do to make him happy, he brushed her off, saying he was too busy for such concerns.

He was always too busy, it seemed. He was a silversmith who made fine trinkets for the wealthy of Alexandria. It was his artistic spirit, his fine eye for detail that had made her fall in love with him back in Antinoopolis. He had made her a little brooch once with a bird on it that was so lifelike she could almost feel its tiny chest rise and fall in her fingers when she held it.

They had been so happy in Antinoopolis. She wished that her uncle had never suggested that they move to the big city where a man like Sarapion could win a fortune with his skilled hands. And true, a man like Sarapion could win a fortune there, but not when the markets were crowded with hundreds of other equally talented young men like Sarapion who had all come to Alexandria chasing their futile dreams. Though he did amazing work, there was a glut of such trinkets and he was often forced to sell them for much cheaper than they were worth. Many days he barely broke even, and what little he made after rent and food and taxes was usually squandered on wine and gambling and whores. Artemesia had followed him one night, curious to discover where her husband was spending all his time and their money. She found him in the arms of a whore; not even a beautiful courtesan, mind you, but a dirty old hag pressed up against the wall in a dingy alleyway. She struck the woman and spat in her face before Sarapion managed to pull her off. He beat her, then sent her home to wait for him. When he came back he was dully apologetic and promised that it wouldn't happen again. Things had been rough at work and he was just looking for a little release. It was just sex: there had been no love in it. And the whole time that he was talking, all Artemesia could think of was the smell of the old whore on him.

She didn't speak to him for a week. At first he made half-hearted attempts to patch things up, but then he fell into his own morose silence and ignored her after that. It took another couple months before things regained any sort of semblance of their previous life, but it was a semblance only. Before too long Sarapion was staying later and later at work, and some nights he didn't come home at all. When he did he always stank of wine and whores, and more times than not she suffered beatings at his hands.

Artemesia was miserable. She knew no one here in Alexandria and she missed her family back in Antinoopolis. At first she wrote them letters and looked forward to hearing news of her cousins and old friends back home, but as she slipped deeper and deeper into misery her letters grew less frequent until she stopped writing altogether. Every once in a while she still got letters from her family asking about her health and begging her to come visit, but she threw them away unanswered. What could she tell these people who loved her? How could she tell them how horrible her life had become, how much she longed for death? They wouldn't understand. Her mother had endured the same or worse from her father. She would just tell her to endure, to be strong and take it like a woman. They were proud Greeks, from one of the best, if not one of the wealthiest, old families of Antinoopolis. Lesser-class women might freely divorce their families, but not women like her mother's people.

And that's why Artemesia had come out here on this moonless night. Outside the filth and clamor of Alexandria there was another city, populated by the dead. She found the stillness of the mausoleums and the humble stelai reassuring. The only signs of life were the wreaths of wilting flowers and the meals left for the dead by their loving families. She wondered if anyone would pour honey and oil out for her, leave behind bread and eggs for her weary soul to eat when she was gone. Probably not. The only person who knew her here was Sarapion and it was clear that he no longer cared. He probably wouldn't even miss her, except that there would be no one to cook him dinner or clean his hovel once she was gone.

Artemesia sat down on an offering table in front of one of the larger mausoleums in the necropolis and shivered. The marble was cold from the chill night air, and she momentarily regretted not bringing her mother's wrap again. It would have been warmer, but it reminded her too much of the better days in Antinoopolis, those happy days early in her marriage, and somehow that didn't seem appropriate for what she was about to do.

She unwrapped the knife she had brought with her and held it in her hands, admiring the lovely design of the handle. It was some of Sarapion's best work. He had originally made it for a wealthy client, but admired it too much to hand it over to someone who would never appreciate the delicate artistry that had gone into its construction. Somehow it seemed appropriate that Sarapion's favorite piece would be the instrument of her destruction.

Artemesia ran her finger along its cool edge and drew blood. It was sharp and that made her smile. She had suffered enough already. Artemesia let out a deep sigh and readied herself for death.

"Pretty night, isn't it?"

The knife fell from her nerveless fingers and clattered to the ground below.

Artemesia spun around, almost toppling off of the offering table to see who was there with her.

The necropolis was empty, just shadows and the monuments of the dead.

"Who are you?" Artemesia blurted out, fear gripping her throat. "Show yourself." It would have been a command, but her voice faltered midway through.

In the distance a hound bayed at the moonless night's sky. A moment later, closer, a screech owl's hoot tore apart the silence. Artemesia shivered uncontrollably. She reached down and picked up the knife, holding it now as a weapon in front of her.

When her eyes rose once more she saw that she was no longer alone.

With just the dim light of the stars overhead, she could make out the figure of the tall, beautiful woman who was standing before her. She was clothed in a saffron robe and tall hunting boots. Hair the color of a raven's wing spilled down her bone-white shoulders and she wore a crescent moon crown upon her broad forehead. Her lips were dark as blood and her features sharp but comely, her age impossible to determine. Her eyes were strange, however. A trick of the shadows, perhaps, but it seemed that they were entirely black, without any hint of white to them. They were cold and severe, the eyes of an inhuman creature, but they held no malice for Artemesia, that much she could tell.

"Is that a gift for me?" The strange woman asked, nodding to the blade Artemesia held trembling in front of her.

Artemesia glanced down and lowered the blade. Somehow she didn't think it would do any good against the strange woman.

"No. I ... I have other plans for it."

"Ah, I see." The woman smiled and it sent a chill through Artemesia's whole body. "So I have interrupted you then?"

"Yes."

"I am sorry. I shall be on my way again."

She turned to go, and Artemesia almost let her, but then some part of her called out, "Stop. Wait." before she even realized that she was speaking. "Why are you here?"

"This is my home." The woman smiled again, and shrugged her arms. The gesture seemed to encompass the whole of the necropolis. "It wasn't always, but since you people came to this land, this is the place where you seek me out the most."

"Who are you?"

"Don't you know that already?"

Artemesia paused for a moment. It seemed that she should recognize the other woman, but she did not. "No, I don't know you."

"Pity." Another icy smile.

The woman knelt by a crudely chiseled stele, her movement fluid and graceful, and she picked up a loaf of bread and some garlic and then stood. She offered her treasures to Artemesia. "Hungry?"

"What are you doing? Don't touch that! It's food for the dead!"

"It is my food as well." The woman bit into the garlic and chewed quietly.

"But it's profane. How can you eat that?"

"I eat all that is cast off. The filth, the rot, the spoiled and damaged things. What men hate and wish to get rid of — belongs to me." She tore off a chunk of the stale bread, and Artemesia could see that it was wormy and mold-covered from having sat out for so long. The strange woman ate it silently, appreciatively, as if she were dining on quail meat and delicate sweet-treats.

"Who are you? A ghost? A demon?"

"Some say so." She picked up a jar of wine left on another tomb and proceeded to wash down her meal. "But they are wrong. The spirits follow in my train and I am their mistress." She smiled and licked the wine from her lips. The gesture reminded Artemesia of a hound wiping blood from its muzzle.

"Why are you here?"

"This is my home." The woman gently set the now empty wine-jar down and came to stand in front of Artemesia. "And I am here for you."

"Me?" Artemesia swallowed hard. She was suddenly very afraid.

"Yes. May I sit here?" She nodded to the space on the offering table next to Artemesia. She thought of refusing, of getting up and fleeing into the safety of the darkness — but then she thought better of it. She doubted anywhere would be safe with this woman hunting her. She moved over to make room and said, "Sure."

The woman took her seat, but Artemesia did not feel the weight of a body next to her. Her flesh crawled and every instinct in her body screamed to rise and run. Instead she stayed put and said, "Why?"

"You called out to me in your pain and desperation."

"I didn't say anything."

"I hear even when no words are spoken."

"I don't believe that. No one hears me. No one cares."

"I do."

"Why?"

"It's what I do."

"Then you know what I've been through, what I left behind?"

"Yes."

"Why did that happen to me?"

The woman smiled sadly. "Because you were weak and let it happen."

163

Anger rose in Artemesia's heart. How could she say that? She didn't want this. It wasn't her fault. She hadn't asked to move to this horrible city. Didn't decide to be beaten and neglected by her husband. And what could she have possibly done to stop him when he was so much stronger than her? She said as much to the other woman.

"There are ways. There are always ways. You just have to be willing to seek them out. The ways are not always easy. Sometimes it costs you greatly to follow them. But they are there and the choice is always yours to make."

"I do not understand."

"Perhaps not. But you will in time."

The two sat in silence for a while, Artemesia pondering the other woman's strange words. Then she said, "I thought he loved me."

"He did, once. Perhaps he still does, in some small way. Will you trade your happiness for his love, though?"

"I don't understand. What are you suggesting?"

"You came here to die tonight, did you not?"

Artemesia nodded, suddenly shamed by the admission.

"Why? You could just leave him, divorce him."

"Where would I go? What would I do? No man would have me now."

"There is more to life than men, dear."

"That is easy for you to say. You are ... whatever you are."

The woman smiled at that.

"I have no skills, no home. I'd be on the streets and starve. Or have to become a whore."

"Perhaps. Perhaps not. But you wouldn't really know unless you tried. You never know what you're capable of until it comes down to it."

"I am tired and I hurt. I don't want to hurt anymore."

"I understand. As I said, all that is broken and discarded belongs to me. You belong to me."

Artemesia's eyes went wide. The woman sounded crazed ... and yet, somehow, she sensed truth in the words.

"Who are you?"

"You know me already."

She did, but the weight of the realization was too heavy and she dared not speak it aloud.

"What am I to do?"

"I cannot say that, dear child. I merely show you the paths that cross. You must choose which of them to take."

"But what if I choose wrongly?"

"There is always that risk. The choice must still be made."

Silence settled upon the necropolis again. When Artemesia's thoughts grew too heavy she turned back to address the strange woman again, but she was alone.

Artemesia set the beautiful knife down where the woman had rested moments before, a gift to the mistress of the cross-roads, and then rose herself and left the dwelling-place of the dead. As she walked home along the dirty streets of sleepless Alexandria she remained uncertain of what she was going to do — but one thing she knew was that she didn't want to end up in that place just yet.

Crossroads

by Melia Suez

A bowl of water,
the sea in miniature.
A small rock,
a piece of earth.
Smoke of incense
tracing the sky.
These are her realms.
Crossroads are not
always paths or roads.
A play yard puddle.
A sea cliff.
A river bridge.
These are subtle
yet crossroads still.
Birth
Puberty
Death
More crossroads
internal and personal.
Whenever there is change,
wherever there is transition,
There she is found.
Hekate

Hecate's Rising

by Brian Seachrist & Lori Newlove

Midnight at the Crossroads,
Black cat across my path
A man is hanging from the gallows,
Bound by the misdeeds in his past
Thick fog lies damp and heavy
The smell of sulphur hangs in the air
Don't know what She's got in store for me
But I'm feeling just a little bit scared

'Cause Hecate Is Rising
Hecate Is Rising
Hecate Is Rising
Hecate Is Rising

She calls to me from the shadows
She says:
"Child, come on down here.
I'm gonna show you what you got inside
I'm gonna make you face your fear.
You've heard all the stories about Me
I'm here to tell you they're all true
Better keep your wits about you fool
'Cause I'm coming after you."

'Cause Hecate Is Rising
Hecate Is Rising
Hecate Is Rising
Hecate Is Rising

"You can run from Me but I will follow.
You can't hide from me – sometime night must fall,
And if you deny Me, I will hunt you down,
Swim, slither, creep, jump, fly, run, walk or crawl!"

Look into My mirror,
(I don't want to see)
You've already come this far
(These things just cannot be)

167

I know you won't like what you see
(I don't want to believe)
But you know it's who you really are.
(NO, NO, NO!!!!)
"Yesssssss"

'Cause Hecate Is Rising
Hecate Is Rising
Hecate Is Rising
Hecate Is Rising

I know my time is coming soon
I've lifted the last veil
But I've got Hecate by my side
She'll be my guide in Hell
Yeah, Hecate is rising

Hecate is Rising
Hecate Is Rising
Hecate Is Rising
Hecate Is Rising

We are We who are They,
We are They who are We
We are the whispering wind of fate
We are One who is Three

We are We who are They,
We are They who are We
We are the whispering wind of fate
We are Hecate!

Gatekeepers, Way-Clearers, Mediators: Wepwawet (or Anubis and Hermanubis), Hekate, and Ianus in the Practices of the Ekklesía Antínoou

by P. Sufenas Virius Lupus

The Ekklesía Antínoou is a queer, Graeco–Roman–Egyptian syncretist reconstructionist polytheist group dedicated to Antinous, the deified lover of the Roman Emperor Hadrian. Historically, the cultus' origin dates to late 130 C.E., and the specific location which it first began was the site of the future city of Antinoöpolis in Egypt (which was then called Hir-Wer, which had a small settlement called Besa beforehand), because of the drowning of Antinous in the Nile near that location, which granted immortality to its victims in Egyptian belief. However, Antinous himself was of Arcadian Greek descent, having been born in Bithynion-Claudiopolis (near Bolu in modern Turkey), a colony of Mantineia, in the Roman province of Pontus-Bithynia on the coast of the Black Sea in Asia Minor. And, of course, despite being a philhellene, the Emperor himself was Roman, with a family originating in Spain. The cultus ended up spreading quite widely across the Empire, into Italy and the city of Rome itself, but it was particularly popular in the Greek East, and Antinoöpolis remained a vital and interesting city religiously for many centuries.

Thus, the historical heritage of the modern Ekklesía Antínoou is Egyptian, Greek, and Roman, and this heritage is recognized at the beginning of every major public ritual of the group, no matter what the occasion or the content of the ritual happens to be.[1] Before the opening acclamations and procession of the image of Antinous in any ritual, invocations are said to the deities Wepwawet, Hekate, and Ianus (in that order) to recognize the seniority of the religious traditions standing behind the emergence of the cultus of Antinous. While Egyptian culture did flourish long before the other two, and Greek culture also had its centuries in the sun before being eclipsed by Rome, the specific order here also refers to the circumstances surrounding Antinous' death and its particular link to deification from Egypt, the boy's birth in Bithynia and his upbringing and heritage in Greek culture, and finally his association to the Roman Emperor and the imperial cultus, which was the reason for the success and spread of his cultus (at least initially). It is almost as if the idea of past-present-future in this construction equates to death being in the past (for the past is, indeed, dead), birth in the present (for the present is always being born), and life and love in the future (for what do both life and love yearn for other than their continuation into infinity?). Further, the male (animal-headed) form of Wepwawet, the female form of Hekate, and the often bisexual[2] form of two-headed Ianus[3] encompasses a great deal (though by no means all) of the gender diversity of the modern membership of the Ekklesía Antínoou. Much more could be said about this formulation symbolically and theologically, but the present discussion is concerned with other particularities.

One difficulty that might arise in people's minds over this practice is that Wepwawet, Hekate, and Ianus are not attested in any known archaeological artifacts, inscriptions, or literary texts in close association with Antinous. Therefore, it might be asked: how did these associations emerge, and what is the purpose of maintaining them? In honor of the present anthology's dedication, the majority of this discussion will focus on Hekate, but a brief treatment of Wepwawet and Ianus before proceeding to our goddess honorand would be useful for the sake of thoroughness.

Wepwawet is a very ancient Egyptian deity whose name means "Opener of the Ways," who is portrayed as jackal-headed. While there are other deities in Egypt that are likewise portrayed, the most commonly recognized one is Anubis, the son of Osiris and Nephthys, who was subsequently the god most associated with embalming, and as time went on, the psychopomp function of the latter blended with the "way-opening" of the former.[4] Plutarch's *On Isis and Osiris* 14 gives a curious story as to why the canine association attended the deity: because his mother had exposed him in fear of Set/Typhon, and when Isis sought him out to assist in her search for Osiris with the help of dogs, Anubis subsequently became her guardian just as dogs guard men.[5] Anubis was subsequently often grouped with Serapis, Isis, and Harpocrates in the later Graeco-Roman-Egyptian cultus to Serapis and Isis, and syncretized forms of Anubis emerged in combination with Hermes Psychopompos, becoming Hermanubis.[6] The later Christian saint Christopher was also portrayed as cynocephalic, was celebrated on July 25th (the festival of Hermanubis), and in fact it is possible that his name etymologizes as Christ oupherou, "Christ's way-opener," hearkening back to the roots of this figure in Wepwawet.[7] There is one Egyptian tomb painting, the so-called "Tondo of the Two Brothers," which was found in Antinoöpolis, which depicts two men, each of whom has a deity (possibly their patron?) over one of his shoulders. The younger man has Osirantinous over his shoulder, while the older has Hermanubis.[8] As a way-opener and psychopomp, the figures of Wepwawet, Anubis, and Hermanubis (conceived as one cynocephalic being or as separate individual deities) make excellent deities to invoke initially in any Ekklesía Antínoou rituals.

170

Ianus is fairly well recognized amongst modern people as the two-headed or two-faced deity of ancient Rome under the name "Janus," and his name contains the root of the word janitor (i.e. a door-keeper), and the month-name January. Ovid's *Fasti* 1.63-288 explains a number of ancient Roman associations with the deity, including why the new year begins during his month, why he has multiple faces, and why offerings are made to him first of all in rituals.[9] In Ekklesía Antínoou reckoning, three important holidays fall within the month of January. On January 1st, the death of Aelius Caesar, the first adopted heir of the Emperor Hadrian, is observed, despite Hadrian's wishes not to mark the occasion or offer him deification[10] (which does not seem to have stopped many people later in history from reckoning him deified). On January 24th, Hadrian's *dies natalis* (birthdate) is celebrated.[11] Finally, late in the month, on January 29th, the first appearance of the star of Antinous in 131 C.E. (about three months after his death) is celebrated, as this date has been revealed by examination of Chinese astronomical records.[12] The order of these dates, interestingly, supports the idea of "past, present, future" mentioned previously, as represented by the death festival of Divus Aelius Caesar, the birth of Divus Hadrianus, and then the continuing presence and hope offered by the star of Antinous. As all of these take place within the month in which Ianus is most honored, giving him a share of ongoing honors by the Ekklesía Antínoou also makes logical sense, apart from the Roman customs which would give him this privilege in any case.

Now, at last, to the great goddess Hekate. Interestingly, Hekate has relations to the other two deities mentioned previously, and thus acts as an excellent intermediate or bridging figure in the order in which the three deities are invoked in ritual. Hekate is related to Anubis by Plutarch in *On Isis and Osiris* 44 in an intriguing passage, which I give here in full:

When Nephthys gave birth to Anubis, Isis treated the child as if it were her own; for Nephthys is that which is beneath the Earth and invisible, Isis that which is above the Earth and visible; and the circle which touches these, called the horizon, being common to both, has received the name Anubis, and is represented in form like a dog; for the dog can see with his eyes both by night and by day alike. And among the Egyptians Anubis is thought to possess this faculty, which is similar to that which Hekate is thought to possess among the Greeks, for Anubis is a deity of the lower world as well as a god of Olympus. Some are of the opinion that Anubis is Kronos. For this reason, inasmuch as he generates all things out of himself and conceives all things within himself, he has

171

gained the appellation of "Dog." There is, therefore, a certain mystery observed by those who revere Anubis; in ancient times the dog obtained the highest honors in Egypt; but, when Cambyses had slain the Apis and cast him forth, nothing came near the body or ate of it save only the dog; and thereby the dog lost his primacy and place of honor above that of all the other animals.[13]

Hekate is connected to dogs from a very early period in Greek culture,[14] and thus this connection between Anubis and Hekate makes sense in other manners as well as those outlined here. The idea that Hekate, like Anubis, has a share in chthonic as well as celestial realms is found as early as Hesiod's passage from the *Theogony* 411-452, in which Hekate is said to have been honored by Zeus above all others, and to have been given a share of the land, the sea, and the sky, and that she had a share due to her from all who came forth from earth and sky.[15] Thus, it would be sensible for any deity who has both chthonic and celestial natures − as Antinous does − to also acknowledge these other deities who likewise share such spheres of influence!

Hekate is further related to Ianus in a number of instances from classical literature. Ovid's *Fasti* 1.89-144 mentions the two together at one point toward the end of this section, particularly in Hekate's aspect as three-faced and the appearance of Ianus Bifrons ("two-faced," called here *biformis*),[16] in his explanation for the reasons for the deity's double-faced aspect. Further, the fifth century neoplatonist Proclus has a hymn in which he honors Hekate and Ianus together, praising the former as the mother of the gods and guardian of the gates, and the latter as Zeus and the forefather of all.[17] These two multiple-aspected deities, both of whom are connected with or syncretized to the titanic generation of immortals, and for whom beginnings and safe passages are particularly important, could only be expected to become more elevated in status and perceived power as time went on. As a grouping, therefore, Wepwawet, Hekate, and Ianus are very apt for any Graeco-Roman-Egyptian practitioner to consider in their preliminary rites.

Hekate occurs on a number of occasions in a particular text from the corpus of the *Greek Magical Papyri*, specifically *PGM* IV, which has a number of noteworthy Antinoan connections. *PGM* IV was formerly known as the "Great Magical Papyrus of Paris," and is probably a fourth-century C.E. copy of a second-century C.E. original.[18] The two things which most closely connect this composition to an Antinoan context are as follows: a version of one of the spells found therein, lines 296-466,[19] is found with a figurine like the one described in the recipe with a specific invocation of Antinous, probably from the vicinity of Antinoöpolis;[20] and, one of the spells in the papyrus is ascribed to

Pachrates, an Egyptian mage who gave the spell to Hadrian.[21] More will be said about this figure in the discussion to follow below. However, it does remain to see what role Hekate plays in *PGM* IV. On three occasions, the *voces magicae* in a spell read "AKTIOPHIS ERESCHIGAL NEBOUTOSOUALETH,"[22] and Betz notes that Aktiophis is an epithet of Selene, but as Selene, Artemis, and Hekate were syncretized and considered forms of the moon by this stage, it is possible that Hekate gives some of her more fierce associations to the spells concerned; indeed, Betz remarks that this particular formula might specifically refer to Hekate.[23] The formula "ERESCHIGAL NEBOUTOSOUALETH" occurs once in a spell that refers to Hekate specifically.[24] In two further spells, a three-headed figure of Hekate must be created as an ingredient of the spell concerned.[25] While it is impossible to be certain where this papyrus originated, or who the compiler and intended users happened to be, the specific occurrence of the AKTIOPHI ERESCHIGAL NEBOUTOSOUALETH formula in Pachrates' spell, plus the occurrence of Hekate in general, and Hekate as an equivalent/syncretism of Selene, is of particular interest for Antinoan purposes.

In an interesting fragmentary Antinoan text from c. 285 C.E., from the *Oxyrynchus Papyri*, and discovered in about 1993, comes a section discussing the lion hunt of Hadrian and Antinous (on which more in a moment), and also Antinous' deification. This fragment includes the idea that Antinous' deification took place in a manner parallel to that of Endymion, when it says that Selene, "upon more brilliant hopes bade him shine as a star-like bridegroom and garlanding the night like with a circle she took him for her husband."[26] There is some evidence to indicate that other deified imperial figures associated with the Hadrianic regime – specifically, his sister Aelia Domitia Paulina – was syncretized to Selene in certain instances.[27] The remembrance of other members of the Hadrianic and Traianic imperial families in the *demoi*-names of Antinoöpolis was established from the earliest times of the city's founding,[28] Hadrian's foundation of which being noted immediately after the passage above.[29] J. R. Rea's notes on this passage even suggest that chthonic Hekate's role in deification of mortals may be alluded to in this syncretism with Selene.[30] Antinous' connection to Diana (the Roman goddess often syncretized with Artemis, likewise syncretized to Luna, the functional equivalent of Selene) at a particular cult at Lanuvium near Rome is also known,[31] and is highly suggestive in the present case.[32]

But this is only the tail end, as it were, of that particular narrative section of the poem concerned. The previous portion of the poem discusses the lion hunt of Hadrian and Antinous, culminating in its various mythological allusions and discussion of the lotus-miracle emerging from the event with the words "into the Nile he hurried for purification of the blood of the lion...."[33] The lotus miracle is mentioned in a prose piece from a papyrus found at Tebtynis,[34] and the lion hunt is treated in a number of other locations, including a further papyrus fragment from Oxyrynchus, giving more details on the actual hunt,[35] as well as sculpturally on the hunting tondo now on the arch of Constantine in Rome,[36] but most importantly for present purposes, in a passage from Athenaeus' *Deipnosophistae* ("The Learned Banqueters") 15.677, in which the origin of the poetic tradition on these matters is credited to one Pancrates, an Egyptian poet.[37] This Pancrates is conjectured to be the same person as the Pachrates referred to in the *PGM* IV text as having given the particular spell there to Hadrian, and he may likewise be the same figure as the Egyptian priest Pancrates referred to in Lukian of Samosata's *Philopseudes* ("Lover of Lies"), a satirical text which is the earliest occurrence of the "sorcerer's apprentice" motif.[38] In other writings, Lukian alludes to the Antinoan cultus in a less-than-flattering light,[39] and thus this particular appearance of Pancrates in a text showing how supposed magicians and those with esoteric knowledge prey upon the witless would be a further commentary on the perception of the Antinoan cultus, with its miracles involving lions and lotuses, the star which was said to be Antinous' katasterism, and the overabundant inundation of the Nile in 131 which was attributed to Antinous' death.[40] Hekate and her epiphany plays a large role elsewhere in Lukian's *Philopseudes,* and the narration of her epiphany is likewise attributed to Eucrates, the character in the frame-tale who also interacted with Pancrates.[41] The connection of *PGM* IV to Hekate generally, and particularly in Pachrates' spell therein, and likewise the connection between Pancrates as the final (and epitomizing) tale in the *Philopseudes* and Hekate's appearances therein as well, is nothing if not suggestive.

But, even more interesting in relation to Hekate is a lost text (or texts) dating from some decades after the origins of the Antinoan cultus, namely, the *Chaldean Oracles,* a late second-century C.E. corpus which survive in fragments from various commentaries on the corpus from the mid-third century onwards, and well into the Christian period.[42] In fragment 147, found in the commentary of the eleventh-century C.E. Michael Psellus' work, the epiphany of Hekate is said to come with a darkening of the heavens (both the lights of stars and moon), earthquakes and lightning, and that "you will observe all things in the form of a lion" (*athréseis pánta léonta*).[43] The other characteristics of this epiphany are echoed in the epiphany of Hekate in Lukian's *Philopseudes* mentioned earlier.[44] In the manner via which Antinous is said to have slain the lion, purified its blood in the Nile (which became the red Nile lotus thereafter named for Antinous), and then gone on to his deification through Selene in the Oxyrynchus papyrus from c. 285 C.E. discussed above, the fact that Pancrates/Pachrates is probably the source of this particular bit of theological mythology, and that Hekate is intimately connected with what can be reconstructed of Pancrates/Pachrates' overall magical and religious milieu, I cannot help but think that it is possible that Hekate's epiphany as a lion might also play into the overall construction of this mytheme.[45]

Of the three gatekeeper, way-clearer and mediator deities reckoned in Ekklesía Antínoou ritual practice and devotion, connections of them to Antinous' ancient cultus are difficult to reconstruct with any certainty; but of these, the most intriguing and compelling case can be made for Hekate, for all of the reasons previously explained. However, as we are reconstructionists, and actual practices on the ground are also impossible to know with any certainty, it is just as well to claim modern interest and appeal for these deities to be included in rituals, and to honor them in preliminary rites on festival occasions. It should be the task of everyone involved in reconstructed traditions to not only research attested ancient practices with diligence and discernment, but also to create new practices which will infuse the old traditions with new life, relevant for people in the modern world, because it is in the modern world – and always in *the present* (whether the eternal present of myth or the temporal present of our daily lives and experiences) – that ritual and devotion takes place. Even if Pancrates/Pachrates were to be called up from the dead and interviewed on these matters, and if his answers to the specific points of this discussion all happened to be met with negatives, ridicule, and derision, the theological formulations and mythic constructions of the early twenty-first century are no more nor less authentic and useful than the users of them find them to be. And how appropriate, therefore, that of the three deities, perhaps representing the past, the present, and the future, that the mediating term of the three, Hekate, is the one also representing the temporal present, and the one who, even in absence, seems to be the most present in the mythos of Antinous.

---

[1] Some holidays, feasts, and celebrations in the group are specifically Antinoan in nature; others are versions of historically-attested festivals from ancient Mediterranean cultures, like the Lupercalia, Serapeia, or other such occasions.

[2] "Bisexual" is here understood in the gender rather than sexual orientation sense; while this is a more antiquated usage, "hermaphroditic" or "intersexed" are also not quite appropriate terms for description of this form and understanding of the deity.

[3] Macrobius, *Saturnalia* 1.9.8; see Percival Vaughan Davies (trans.), *Macrobius, The Saturnalia*, Records of Civilization, Sources and Studies 79 (London and New York: Columbia University Press, 1969), p. 67.

4 For some information on this, see Terence DuQuesne, *Anubis, Upwawet, and Other Deities: Personal Worship and Official Religion in Ancient Egypt* (Cairo: The Egyptian Museum Cairo/Supreme Council of Antiquities Press, 2007).

5 Frank Cole Babbitt (trans.), *Plutarch, Moralia, Volume V* (Cambridge: Harvard University Press, 1936, reprint 2003), pp. 38-39.

6 Jean-Claude Grenier, *Anubis Alexandrin et Romain* (Leiden: E. J. Brill, 1977), particularly pp. 53-59 on Hermes-Anubis/Hermanubis.

7 David Gordon White, *Myths of the Dog-Man* (Chicago and London: University of Chicago Press, 1991), pp. 43-44.

8 Ann E. Haeckl, "Brothers or Lovers? A New Reading of the 'Tondo of the Two Brothers'," *Bulletin of the American Society of Papyrologists* 38 (2001), pp. 63-78 and Plate 6.

9 Sir James George Frazer (trans.), *Ovid, Fasti* (Cambridge: Harvard University Press, 1931), pp. 6-23.

10 Anthony R. Birley, *Hadrian the Restless Emperor* (London and New York: Routledge, 2000), pp. 292-294.

11 Mary Beard, John North, and Simon Price (eds./trans.), *Religions of Rome, Volume 2: A Sourcebook* (Cambridge: Cambridge University Press, 1998, reprint 2001), p. 72, which is an early third century military calendar from Dura Europus recording the *dies natalis* of Aelius Caesar on January 13 and that of Hadrian on the 24th; see also an Egyptian calendar fragment from Tebtynis, in S. Eitrem and Leiv Amundsen (eds.), *Papyri Osloenses*, Vol. 3 (Oslo: The Academy of Science and Letters at Oslo, 1936), pp. 54-55, which records both dates as well.

12 J. R. Rea (ed./trans.), *The Oxyrynchus Papyri*, Vol. 63 (London: Egypt Exploration Society, 1996), pp. 14-15.

13 Babbitt, pp. 106-107.

14 On this, see Dr. Phillip A. Bernhardt-House's essay elsewhere in the present volume.

15 Glenn W. Most (trans.), *Hesiod, Theogony, Works and Days, Testimonia* (Cambridge: Harvard University Press, 2006), pp. 36-39.

16 Frazer, pp. 8-13.

17 Frederick C. Grant, *Hellenistic Religions: The Age of Syncretism*, Library of Liberal Arts 134 (Indianapolis and New York: The Liberal Arts Press/The Bobbs-Merrill Company, Inc., 1953), p. 172.

18 Daniel Ogden, *Night's Black Agents: Witches, Wizards and the Dead in the Ancient World* (London and New York: Hambledon Continuum, 2008), p. 116.

19 Hans Dieter Betz (ed./trans.), *The Greek Magical Papyri in Translation including the Demotic Spells, Volume One: Texts*, Second Edition, with an updated bibliography (Chicago: University of Chicago Press, 1992; paperback edition 1996). Further references to this work in the present article are hereafter indicated by *PGM* followed by papyrus number, lines, and pages of Betz' edition. An alternate translation, with commentary, of this spell is found in Daniel Ogden, *Magic, Witchcraft,*

and *Ghosts in the Greek and Roman Worlds: A Sourcebook* (Oxford and New York: Oxford University Press, 2002), pp. 247-250 §239.

[20] John G. Gager, *Curse Tablets and Binding Spells from the Ancient World* (New York and Oxford: Oxford University Press, 1999), pp. 97-100 §28; Beard, North, and Price, pp. 266-267 §11.5a; Ogden, *Magic, Witchcraft*, pp. 250-251 §240.

[21] *PGM* IV, 2441-2621, pp. 82-86.

[22] *PGM* IV, 2441-2621, p. 83, lines 2483-2486; 2708-2784, pp. 89-90, lines 2745-2753; 2891-2942, p. 93, lines 2912-2915.

[23] Betz, p. 337 s.v. NEBOUTOSOUALETH.

[24] *PGM* IV, 1390-1495, p. 65, lines 1417-1420.

[25] *PGM* IV, 2006-2125, p. 75, lines 2119-2123; 2785-2890, p. 92, lines 2880-2884.

[26] Rea, p. 10.

[27] Günter Grimm, "Paulina und Antinous. Zure Vergöttlichung der Hadriansschwester in Äegypten," in Christoph Börker and Michael Donderer (eds.), *Das antike Rom und der Osten: Festschrift für Klaus Parlasca zum 65. Geburtstag* (Erlangen: Universitätsbund Erlanden-Nürnberg e. V.,1990), pp. 33-44.

[28] Mary Taliaferro Boatwright, *Hadrian and the Cities of the Roman Empire* (Princeton and Oxford: Princeton University Press, 2000), p. 194 note 124.

[29] Rea, p. 10.

[30] Rea, p. 13 note 11.

[31] Beard, North, and Price, pp. 292-294 §12.2.

[32] I have treated this topic more extensively elsewhere; see "Artemis and the Cult of Antinous," in Thista Minai *et al.* (eds.), *Unbound: A Devotional Anthology for Artemis* (Eugene: Bibliotheca Alexandrina, 2009), pp. 106-112.

[33] Rea, p. 10.

[34] Achille Vogliano (ed.), *Papiri della R. Universita di Milano*, Volume 1 (Milan: Ulrico Hoepli, 1937), pp. 175-183 at 176-179. See also the "poetic" translation of this text in my book, *The Phillupic Hymns* (Eugene: Bibliotheca Alexandrina, 2008), pp. 54-55 and 260 (notes).

[35] Arthur S. Hunt (ed./trans.), *The Oxyrynchus Papyri*, Vol. 8 (London: Egypt Exploration Society, 1911), pp. 73-77, which is conjectured to be a fragment of Pancrates' actual poem. See also D. L. Page (ed./trans.), *Select Papyri III: Literary Papyri, Poetry* (Cambridge: Harvard University Press, 1957), pp. 516-519.

[36] Mary Taliaferro Boatwright, *Hadrian and the City of Rome* (Princeton and Oxford: Princeton University Press, 1987), p. 190-202.

[37] Charles Burton Gulick (ed./trans.), *Athenaeus, Depinosophistae, Volume 7* (Cambridge: Harvard University Press, 1941), pp. 126-129.

[38] Ogden, *Magic, Witchcraft*, pp. 54-55 §54; *In Search of the Sorcerer's Apprentice: The Traditional Tales of Lucian's Lover of Lies* (Swansea: The

Classical Press of Wales, 2007), pp. 60-61, 231-270; *Night's Black Agents*, pp. 95, 98, 122-123.

[39] Royston Lambert, *Beloved and God: The Story of Hadrian and Antinous* (New York: Viking, 1984), pp. 94, 96, 192; A. M. Harmon (ed./trans.), *Lucian, Volume V* (Cambrdige: Harvard University Press, 1962), pp. 426-433 ("The Parliament of the Gods"); M. D. MacLeod (ed./trans.), Lucian, Volume VII (Cambrdige: Harvard University Press, 1962), pp. 268-281 ("Dialogues of the Gods: Zeus and Hera"), and 281-291 ("Dialogues of the Gods: Zeus and Ganymede"), the latter of which has never been discussed as a possibility of further Antinoan allusion.

[40] I hope to treat this topic further in the future, but I would note that the near-flood caused by the misuse of the spell learned by the character taught by Pancrates in this narrative might mirror the excessive, and even destructive, flooding of the Nile that followed Antinous' death. For evidence of this flooding, see Bernard P. Grenfell and Arthur S. Hunt (ed./trans.), *The Oxyrynchus Papyri*, Vol. 3 (London: Egypt Exploration Society, 1903), pp. 180-183; Eitrem and Amundsen, pp. 55-61.

[41] Ogden, *Magic, Witchcraft*, pp. 272-273 §275; *In Search of the Sorcerer's Apprentice*, pp. 54-56, 161-170.

[42] See Sarah Iles Johnston, *Hekate Soteira: A Study of Hekate's Roles in the Chaldean Oracles and Related Literature* (Atlanta: Scholars Press, 1990), pp. 1-12.

[43] Ruth Majercik, *The Chaldean Oracles: Text, Translation, and Commentary* (Leiden: E. J. Brill, 1989), pp. 104-105 §147, and commentary on p. 196. Hans Lewy, *Chaldean Oracles and Theurgy* (Paris: Études Augustiniennes, 1978), pp. 94 and note 114, discusses this fragment, but believes the reading is mistaken. See also Johnston, pp. 111-112, who agrees with Lewy, and does not accept the text as it stands in Psellus, instead insisting on a textual emendation, because she does not understand how this line could make sense. As should be obvious, I opine that greater credence should be given to the text as it exists, and to the adept commentary on it given by Psellus.

[44] Johnston, p. 116.

[45] While I do not wish to insist upon the point, I'm also reminded of another passage from Plutarch's *On Isis and Osiris* (38), which concerns the connection between the dog-star Sirius and lions observed by the Egyptians, and the rising of the former during the Zodiac month of the latter, which heralds the inundation of the Nile; see Babbitt, pp. 90-93. As Anubis and Hekate seem to share some connection, and Anubis (as well as Hekate) are both said to be cynocephalic, and cynocephali are connected very much to the dog-star, there is the possibility of some synchronism of tradition in that regard. However, more compelling for present purposes is the fact that the inundation of the Nile is attributed to Antinous' miraculous intervention, and therefore its further connection to the lion-month might have been a further factor in Pancrates/Pachrates' theological formulations.

Serpent Hair

by Rebecca Buchanan

serpent-hair
tiny hisses forked tongues
iridescent greens and blues and purples and such reds
gown of mist and moonlight and earth-deep shadows
barefoot down the road
puppy in hand
      left at a crossroad shrine
      suffocated
      favored offering
dogs circling her legs
yipping
barking
running ahead and back
circling running again
and the ghosts who follow
uncounted
a river of pain and fear and denial
angry hungry
hungry for the life never lived
now never to be lived
howling in anguish
answering howl from the dogs
the puppy whines in her hands
serpent-hairs rise and hiss tongues snapping
and the ghosts are silent again
      for a moment
through the night
forever night
never rest

Hermes and Hekate

by Sophie S.

He, she thinks, licking her lips, is everything that she loves about herself. No, no, he is not just that. He is everything that she loves *and* everything that she hates. He is the shadows to cool and comfort her when the light – the bright light that she has grown unaccustomed to in the gloominess of Hades – burns hot-fast-sharp enough to *hurt.* She bleeds for that light; smoke pours from her mouth and eyes, her own power streaming away from her – from her own imbalance.

And thus, when the light stings and her smoke flees, she turns back to the darkness, back to him. He is always there – not pushing, not demanding, just *there.* He opens his arms to accept her; she pushes the low rim of his hat aside and kisses the warm skin of his brow. It shouldn't be possible, not for a god whose very lips are dark with shadow, but he's always warm, as though fire burns under his skin. She loves that; and maybe she hates it a little, too. Maybe she hates him a little.

But in that moment, with her body nestled against his and stealing the warmth from his skin, she does not think of love and hate. No: she thinks, instead, of another lover – her only other. She is of the night, of gloomy death and prophecies of thus; and so perhaps it was natural that she would fall into Hades' bed, one Summer night when they were drunk on their own despair. Summer is Aphrodite's season, after all – her domain does stretch to the Underworld, of course, for she is a goddess of life and, thus, of death – and she had not seen Hermes for almost a month. Time travels differently between the worlds; although she knew that it had been only a month, it had felt like endless, lonely years. Hades, hungry, kissed her first. She remembers that clearly, despite the fogginess of her mind and of their encounter. Passion fueled them, then, but it did not hide how much Hades repelled her, when their chitons were strewn beneath them and all she could feel was his cold, hard body against hers.

But she does not like to think of such times. She kisses Hermes again – lips to lips, this time – and thinks instead of her seduction at this lovely-awful god's hands. He was not cold and indifferent like Hades; instead, he brought her cool skin to quivering life with his hands and tongue. She only has to press her fingers to her tongue to feel the echo of her taste and his combined in her mouth – light and shadow, summer and winter, ice and fire. He has never bored her: she is inexperienced and he is not. She chooses to spend her days in Hades with only shades and barely-there nymphai; and he flies through the air, over the earth and through the seas. She envies him that: he is a messenger, bound to them all, and yet he has more freedom than she – lady of the Underworld, minister to Persephone and one-time lover of Hades – will ever have.

Now, though, Hermes pushes the darkness out of her mind with kisses that set her nerves on fire. He does not ask questions, nor comment, nor laugh at her cold, fevered hands that glide over him, awkward and fumbling as ever. He just kisses her, breathing heat into her body, and she responds as she never did for Hades.

Later, she lifts her head from the ground and looks at him. Her skin is flushed, now; and his is cold and pale. The balance has been restored - and when he leaves, he will be warmed by the sun and the kisses of nymphai and his wife, and she will lose her heat to the creeping cold of the Underworld. But such thoughts are not for now, and so when she looks at him she casts all of her thoughts aside. She – Hekate, queen of ghosts and necromancy, lady of blood and life and death – becomes almost mortal with her open expression and too-moist eyes.

I love you, she thinks, as she always does.

And his lips twitch, as they always do; for he is language, he is thought verbalised – and yet he will not answer her unless she speaks the words aloud. He would not do her such an injustice as to act as though she is beneath him, that her body and mind are his alone to read.

But she will not speak the words herself. To do so would be to become truly mortal, to lose her divinity and yield to the pleasures and pains that Aphrodite and her Erotes bring in their laughing, golden wake. She is not ready for that – not yet – but perhaps, one day, she will be.

Song for Hecate

by Rhiannon Asher

O Lady of the darkest soul of night
Mother of Midnight, Ancient Shadow Queen
Bringer of Visions, give to me the sight
To see the sacred in all living things.
And in cold death, still beauty may I see
When You take back into Yourself
the beauty that was me.

O great Hecate, beneath Your waning moon
I stand dark-hooded on the shadowed road
and face three choices, though all roads lead to You
All stories end at last, untold and told.
O Crone of Wisdom, give to me the sight
To see the dance within all things
of darkness and of light.

O Ancient Lady, Mistress of the Night
You of three faces, Maiden, Mother, Crone
Protector of Witches, dancing with delight
On Your brown Earth, together or alone.
Dark Mother Goddess, give to me the sight
In death, in life, may I behold
Your Mystery dark and bright.

Maternal Hecate

by Allyson Szabo

I was but a child of seven or eight years,
Terrified in the night.
I knew not what I called to, so desperately,
And yet I knew instinctively to call.

The mother of my body lay,
Dark and brooding elsewhere,
Never heeding my fears,
Ignoring the stifled sobs in the night.

The gods, they hear our pleas,
Even when screamed silently.
They hear, and they answer us,
In their own mysterious ways.

I was but a child of seven or eight years,
Terrified in the night.
I called out to god, ignorant and desperate,
Innocent, and hungry for comfort.

The mother of my soul answered,
Bright and warm and full of love,
Wrapping incomprehensibly large arms
Around my trembling being.

I didn't know her name, then.
I simply called her "god."
She heard me crying, and took pity
On a child who had no one to nurture her.

I was but a child of seven or eight years,
Terrified in the night,
When she first touched my yearning mind
And made me her own, unknowing.

The mother of mothers,
Hecate, saffron robed and beauteous,
You have never left me,
Through all the tribulations of my life.

Hymn to Hekate

by Lykeia

Swathed in red is Hekate.
Hooded in red is Hekate.
Red hemmed Artemis lift aloft your burning torch,
And bring the trumpet of the nocturnal hunt.
The flow of life is in the hands of Hekate,
And her burning light guides the way.
Terror-ridden roar of the bull is the trumpets blast,
And the hounds bay in search of their prey.
The beasts of the woods shudder in their homes,
And a scream fills the night air.
None is safe from the nocturnal hunt,
And Hekate guides the host of souls to their new abode.
The light of Hekate does not flicker,
But illuminates the halls of the dead,
And exalts in the company of fair Persephone.
Bloodied red Hekate, we leave your monthly feast,
At the site of your throne.
Red swathed Hekate has all roads lain before her,
And merciful goddess greets those unfortunate to share her plate.
The touch of Hekate is merciful, and in her embrace we depart

A Prayer to Hekate

by Hearthstone

Hekate, sure-stepping maid, watcher at the gate,
honored by mighty Zeus above all others,
fair goddess who walks freely along all paths,
holder of shares in all the worlds. Hekate,
keeper of evil from the home, friend of women,
guardian of children, protector in fear and need.

Hekate, keen-eyed one of whom we know too little,
honored in ancient times at each home's door,
receiver of crossroad offerings, of mothers' prayers,
I ask of you, defend us now as you did then.
I call on you to guard my home, my family,
my children. Kind Hekate, I praise and honor you.

Glorious Hekate, well known by all in times past,
honored today as well in many guises,
on this dark night I pray to you, shining goddess.
Peerless Hekate, I pour out sweet wine to you,
I pray to you: safeguard my home, my household;
watch over my daughters; keep all ill from my door.

Daughter of Night

by Todd Jackson

Ranked first among Thine agonies
That one so lovely should go cowled.

Early March.
Cold rains have crossed California
Then rolled over the Sierras and dipped down upon us,
And six straight days chilled Las Vegas.
These cold rains, then carried East along the high wind,
And did great mischief there;
Snow lies two feet deep and more all up the seaboard.
Back here, back West, the Valley lies refreshed.
At midweek there had been a tight seam of heat inside two cold days,
And Saturday we burst into the seventies.
Tonight, the summit of Mount Charleston,
The high point of Earth in this broad County;
The crooked Moon hangs above, just off the peak of black Night.
Hekate's, the crooked Moon, that slices even Night.

The Moon is framed, off-center, by the silhouetted tips of the
    bristlecone pines,
That sprouted when quick girls still dared bulls at Minos.
No longer even a green blush now within that soft mass;
The pines are but blacker shapes against black Night,
Jagged in the corners of my sight, the stars all hid behind.

While, below, warm spring sunlight has stroked Las Vegas,
Then soothed it with cool winds,
It is white winter here atop Mount Charleston,
Where the cloudwater fell as it would fall two thousand miles east,
As snow.
Winter had entered the valley as a nymph in white taffeta, billowing
    through Night;
She drifted southeast, sailing among the clouds,
Snagged underneath by the tips of all the Sierras,
And above,
Snagged also upon the crooked Moon;
The winter nymph here has paid due tribute
To Hekate,

Then flowed eastward in a shredded gown.
Mount Charleston, as the tall peak, has snagged its own big patch off
    the gown,
And I am standing here, one man among two amid white snow,
And I am black, like Hekate,
And the hounds,
Here, cast against white snow, as
Above, on white moondust. I look now with all my eyes
And behold, the splash of dogprints in the snow.

Io Hekate, Daughter of Night
Ahead, three roads crossing, and She knows the steepest way.
Io Hekate, Daughter of Night
Priced steep is Her wisdom, and only the hard can pay.

For the Moon, and Nevada, are two great concaves toward each other,
Split by black broad space
As great palms outspread in the Night,
So that the Moon, and Nevada, are not aimless wanderers;
They are pinned,
Such that that tight cislunar space has sprung five whirlpools,
And close upon Nevada, encircling the Earth, a skin of gathered
    Sunfire.
I leave bootprints in the snow atop the mountain, as
Above, in that white sliver dangled among distant stars
There are boot prints studded in the Moon dust.

Io Hekate, Daughter of Night
Ahead, three roads crossing, and She knows the steepest way.
Io Hekate, Daughter of Night
Priced steep is Her wisdom, and only the hard can pay.

Hers is the Moon, and especially the crooked Moon.
Hers that part of Dionysos' sap that poisons and heals.
Hers is the jellyfish sting.
And that bright droplet off the rattler's fang,
That inside itself is whirling as it dangles there.
Hers, the thirst for riches, that gives focus to spirit,
Hers, the hymen between salesman and closer,
And the big red X on the board.
Hers, the black and the red of the dice.
Hers, the garlic bulb,
That is poison unto poison itself, and thereby heals.
Hers, my recent trade of blood against poverty,

And that blood pays cheap.
Hers the nuggets still dug deep in the land, unpicked,
Waiting,
And the black oil that is the pressed rot of ancient flesh,
And that pools and surges within the Earth,
Then sails the broad seas in ships more numerous
Than breadcrumbs strewn before an audience of birds,
And all, because it burns.
Hers the honorific, Nigger, that is the curse, and delight, of my people,
The choice of Black, and the weight inside that choice,
That may not now be unchosen. For we now are Hers,
And Her grip will not be broken.
Hers the dark shining in the abyss,
Earth's bowels burst hot through the ocean floor,
Hers the weird dark forests that thrive there,
In the pressure.
Hers the ice and the metal in the Moon.
Hid beneath deep rock, yet there is no hiding
From the torchlight.
Hers, the quarter million miles of cold death.
Hers is that knowing of woman that woman may only know
By knowing herself, and among the herbs.
Hers, the mystique of woman.

I know a lady the color of moonlight on bundled wood.
People are dying in her dreams who aren't dead yet.
That comes afterward, and soon.
I have yet to touch the lady.
One day I shall.

Under Night,
Winding down the mountain road.
My friend and I observe upon the city, art, and blackjack.
She
I cannot long speak of.
She
Is not yet fully speakable in this time.
But down in that great splash of lights below
Mine is not the only candle lit
For Hekate. Yes,
Were She to, with a wave of Her hand,
Snuff the brilliant plumage of the Strip,
And Downtown's yellow-white gleaming,
Were She then to shut down the straggler lights of Summerlin,

Of North Las Vegas,
And leave only candles lit for Gods
The valley floor would at first lie black as the ring of mountains
Before Apollo brings them forth with the morning.
The valley floor would at first lie black,
But in time the eyes would focus, and soon make out
Pricks of light, only several, but definite.
Scattered, and yet a gathering,
Witness to the returning of the time.

It is growing warmer down the slope.
We descend from winter toward spring.
But now two fingers on my right hand are struck cold.
Cold has climbed up my knuckles,
Till taking fingernail to lips, I find it ice.
I remind myself of my good health
Yet cannot not ask, Which does this mean?
Stroke or heart attack?
No. It is that She has taken my hand.
She who comes and goes in dread.

I am honored. I will choose something fine tomorrow
To set before the purple candle.

Io Hekate, Daughter of Night
Ahead, three roads crossing, and She knows the steepest way.
Io Hekate, Daughter of Night
Priced steep is Her wisdom, and only the hard can pay.

"Storms' Queen Hekate"
by Antonella Vigliarolo

Some Epithets and Unfamiliar Terms Explained

Anassa eneroi: "Queen of those below" i.e., the dead.

Brimo: "Angry", "terrifying"; an epithet for various Eleusinian goddesses.

Deipnon: "Dinner"; a monthly ritual carried out in honor of Hekate.

Enodia: "of the wayside."

Hekataion: A statue or altar for Hekate set up outside the house or where three roads meet.

Katabasis: "Descent", especially into the underworld.

Khthonia: "the underworld/earthly goddess."

Kleidophorous: "Key-bearing."

Perseis: "Destroyer."

Phosphoros: "Brightly shining/light-bringer."

Prutania: "of the assembly-hall."

Psychopomp: "Guide of souls."

Soteira: "the Savior goddess."

Trimorphis: "of three forms/shapes."

Trivia: "of three roads."

Select Bibliography

Burkert, Walter. *Greek Religion: Archaic and Classical.* Wiley-Blackwell. 1991.

Crowfoot, Greg. *Crossroads.* Aventine Press. 2005.

d'Este, Sorita. *Hekate Liminal Rites: A Study of the rituals, magic and symbols of the torch-bearing Triple Goddess of the Crossroads.* Avalonia, 2009.

Faraone, Christopher A. and Dirk Obbink. *Magika Hiera: Ancient Greek Magic and Religion.* Oxford University Press 1997.

George, Demetra. *Mysteries of the Dark Moon: The Healing Power of the Dark Goddess.* HarperOne. 1992.

Johnston, Sarah Iles. *Hekate Soteira: A Study of Hekate's Roles in the Chaldean Oracles and Related Literature.* An American Philological Association Book. 1990.

_____ *Restless Dead: Encounters Between the Living and the Dead in Ancient Greece.* University of California Press. 1999.

Kerenyi, Carl. *The Gods of the Greeks.* Thames & Hudson. 1980.

Ogden, Daniel. *Magic, Witchcraft, and Ghosts in the Greek and Roman Worlds: A Sourcebook.* Oxford University Press. 2002.

Rabinowitz, Jacob. *The Rotting Goddess: The Origin of the Witch in Classical Antiquity.* Autonomedia, 1998

Ronan, Stephen. *The Goddess Hekate.* Chthonios. 1992.

Varner, Gary R. *Hecate: The Witches' Goddess.* Unknown Publisher. 2007.

Von Rudloff, Robert. *Hekate in Ancient Greek Religion.* Horned Owl Publishing. 1999.

Some Online Resources

Altar to Hekate:
http://www.soulrebels.com/beth/hekate.html

Hekate, the Dark Goddess:
http://www.angelfire.com/biz/MysticalArts/Hekate.html

Hecate, Goddess of Witchcraft:
http://hekate.timerift.net/hecate.htm

Neos Alexandria temple page for Hekate:
http://neosalexandria.org/hekate.htm

Shrine to Hekate:
http://www.paganinstitute.org/T/hekate.shtml

Theoi.com entry on Hekate:
http://www.theoi.com/Khthonios/Hekate.html

Wikipedia entry on Hekate:
http://en.wikipedia.org/wiki/Hecate

About the Bibliotheca Alexandrina

Ptolemy Soter, the first Makedonian ruler of Egypt, established the library at Alexandria to collect all of the world's learning in a single place. His scholars compiled definitive editions of the Classics, translated important foreign texts into Greek, and made monumental strides in science, mathematics, philosophy and literature. By some accounts over a million scrolls were housed in the famed library, and though it has long since perished due to the ravages of war, fire, and human ignorance, the image of this great institution has remained as a powerful inspiration down through the centuries.

To help promote the revival of traditional polytheistic religions we have launched a series of books dedicated to the ancient gods of Greece and Egypt. The library is a collaborative effort drawing on the combined resources of the different elements within the modern Hellenic and Kemetic communities, in the hope that we can come together to praise our gods and share our diverse understandings, experiences and approaches to the divine.

A list of our current and forthcoming titles can be found on the following page. For more information on the Bibliotheca, our submission requirements for upcoming devotionals, or to learn about our organization, please visit us at *www.neosalexandria.org*.

Sincerely,

The Editorial Board of the Library of Neos Alexandria

Current Titles from the Bibliotheca Alexandrina:

Written in Wine: A Devotional Anthology for Dionysos
Dancing God: Poetry of Myths and Magicks by Diotima
Goat Foot God by Diotima
Longing for Wisdom: The Message of the Maxims by Allyson Szabo
The Phillupic Hymns by P. Sufenas Virius Lupus
Unbound: A Devotional Anthology for Artemis
Waters of Life: A Devotional Anthology for Isis and Serapis
Bearing Torches: A Devotional Anthology for Hekate

Forthcoming Titles from the Bibliotheca Alexandrina:

*Words of Power: A Collection of Modern Greek- and Egyptian-Themed
    Fiction in Honor of Thoth*
Queen of the Great Below: An Ereshkigal Devotional
Megaloi Theoi: A Devotional for the Dioskouroi and Their Families
From Cave to Sky: A Devotional Anthology for Zeus

CPSIA information can be obtained
at www.ICGtesting.com
Printed in the USA
LVOW10s1733060318

568844LV00037B/1040/P